# *Dewitched*

# Dewitched

## WHAT YOU NEED TO KNOW ABOUT THE DANGERS OF WITCHCRAFT AND WICCA

# TIM BAKER

**TRANSIT**
www.TransitBooks.com
A Division of Thomas Nelson, Inc.
www.ThomasNelson.com

*For Ron*

DEWITCHED

© 2004 Tim Baker

Published by Transit Books, a Division of Thomas Nelson, Inc., P.O. Box 141000, Nashville, Tennessee 37214.

Cover Design: Anderson Thomas Design, Nashville, Tennessee

Page Design: Book & Graphic Design, Nashville, Tennessee

Illustrations: Mark Ross

Editorial Staff: Elizabeth Kea, Susan Trotman, Sunny Vann, Julie White, Lori Jones

Transit Brand Manager: Kate Etue

Scriptures quoted from *The Holy Bible, New Century Version,* copyright © 1987, 1988, 1991 by Word Publishing, a Division of Thomas Nelson, Inc. Used by permission.

ISBN 0-8499-4434-1

*Printed and bound in the United States of America*

04 05 06 07 08 PHX 5 4 3 2 1

# ACKNOWLEDGMENTS

*L*ike every author, this book is not entirely mine. In fact, in some places this project belongs more to others than it belongs to me. Some of these people include . . .

*Jacqui* (my wife) who used her incredible writing skill to polish this manuscript and create much of the story in *Dewitched.* Jacqui created space for me to write; and encouraged me along the way. Jacqui, you're the most patient and understanding person I know. I love you! Nicole, Jessica, and Jacob reminded me daily of the importance of simple, childlike faith in Christ. They told jokes, hugged, and encouraged as I wrote. You are amazing children, and I love being your dad. Psalm 126:1-3.

*My church family,* who allow me a long leash to write at home. I'm grateful to *Ben Andrus,* and the entire leadership of *Hope Fellowship* who let me teach and pastor at an amazing church.

*Kate Etue* and her staff at W Publishing have taken my words and clarified them. Kate has been especially patient with several rewrites, changes and queries. Thanks for offering me this project, and letting me make it my own.

*Andrea Christian,* my agent and friend. There are no human words that accurately describe Andrea. However, a few word-creations of my own include Superfantastic, Wonderfullyamazing, and possibly, Powerfullywise. Andrea(!), thanks for reading parts of this book, and giving me extremely helpful advice.

*My parents* who unknowingly raised me in what I consider a multi-faith environment. As I've researched this subject, I've relied on my parents' open mindedness, and willingness to listen to and consider ways to think about their faith. Thanks for helping me know and understand other belief systems, and for encouraging me as I wrote.

*My wife's parents* who always encourage, offer advice,and love constantly. Your help along the way with this project has taught me about persevering beyond human strength. Thanks for the gift of your daughter, and your willingness to believe in me.

*John,* a close friend who I used to think was a crazy conspiracy theorist. As I've researched this book, I've seen the connections too. I think you're right about some pretty important things, and it kind of scares me. Thanks for listening to my ideas, offering your own, and giving me unconditional encouragement through this process.

Many close friends and colleagues. Some of the *students* I attend church with, or who have enrolled in my classes have helped clarify many of my ideas and offered necessary input in my understanding of Witchcraft. *Dr. Scott Hummell,* professor of Biblical Studies at LeTourneau University helped clarify my understanding of ancient Israel and their concept of God. *Ron* (to whom this book is dedicated) offered initial ideas and read the first draft. *Alison Simpson* read the initial story ideas and gave loads of advice.

Most of all, *Jesus.* You *are* the Way. You *are* the Truth. You *are* the Life. Would we have peace without You? Would there be hope? Could we truly love? Thank You for Your presence in our lives. Fill us with Your peace, and give us Your endurance. Without You, we are lost. This book is Yours. Thanks for letting me discover it.

# CONTENTS

# Contents

# INTRODUCTION

*W*e lived on a street where every family had at least three kids, except for Ron's. Ron was an only child and for some reason, many of the kids in the neighborhood were attracted to his house. It could have been his welcoming mom, that the entire second story of his house was packed with toys, or his big backyard. Whatever the reason, Ron's house was important in my growing up years.

At Ron's house we put on our own made-up plays, we fought in make-believe wrestling matches, we drank his mom's homemade Kool Aid, and even had a special friendship ritual: Everyone had to drink out of the same cup. "This is the friendship cup," Ron would say. "You have to leave if you don't drink from this cup." Then we would pass the cup. Ron's house was a place of friendship.

Through the years, Ron and I became Christians. We clung to the youth pastors of our medium-sized United Methodist Church, and grew in our knowledge of Christ and how to live for him. Our youth pastors carefully discipled Ron and me into becoming God-fearing believers.

Like many high-school students, I didn't always take my conversion seriously. Once, I met some guys who practiced astral projection and spell casting. Although I was intrigued, I never could duplicate what they claimed they could do. Still, I thought it was neat to know people like them.

While I experimented outside my Christian beliefs, Ron never wavered. Instead, he hung close to God. It was partly because of Ron's steady influence that I eventually came back to Christ.

Ron and I lost touch when we graduated from high school. I went to study the Bible at a Christian university; Ron faded into my history. I got glimpses of his life from mutual friends. He tried college, but it didn't suit him. Then, he married. I did meet his wife, but eventually lost all contact with him.

Then, about a year ago, I called a mutual friend of Ron's and mine, who stayed in touch with Ron over the years. The news wasn't good: Ron had divorced his wife and fallen out of touch with his children. Homeless, he had spent seven months living in his car and sleeping wherever he could park. Our friend told me Ron had been dependent on alcohol and was a practicing Wiccan. It was one of the most depressing tales I've heard.

Through our mutual friend, I was able to establish contact with Ron. We exchanged e-mail addresses, and because I was going to be visiting near where he lived, we made plans to get together. It took several phone calls to get schedules and directions straight. Finally, we decided to meet at a local mall.

My first glimpse of Ron, standing next to a fountain in a mall in Columbus, Ohio, one year ago was surreal. It was as if time had stopped when we lost contact and transported us to that night. We were a little heavier, both had added a few wrinkles, and both were nervous.

We retraced our history as we munched on French fries and huge chocolate chip cookies and drank Cokes. I can't remember the name of the restaurant, but I remember everything about Ron. It feels so good to see an old friend. Despite our obvious differences—he had a pentagram tattooed on one hand and a dragon (I think it looked like a seahorse) on his arm—our friendship was stronger than I expected. I would have never sat and talked to a Wiccan I didn't know, but it didn't matter what Ron believed. For three hours, we sat and talked. I didn't want to leave. I still loved my friend. And, turns out, he still liked me.

This book is for you, Ron. I love you, man. I still remember the time you hit me with the stick and I socked you in the jaw. Thanks for the friendship cup, and the way we shared it again, a year ago. I don't care about your pentagram or the dragon. Years ago, you stood faithful to Christ in a time when I did not. Now, it's my turn.

My prayer for you is much like the one Mitch prays in this book. I am praying that your eyes will be opened one day. (We all experience blindness). I hope that you will see that you need rescuing. (We've all been lost at least once). And I pray that you will see the amazing arms of Jesus wrapped around you.

I'm looking forward to at least one more friendship cup, and I hope it's not another lifetime before we can share it.

TIM BAKER
April 2004

# PREFACE

When I took this project, I had no idea what was in store for me. I thought I would approach this stuff clinically: a little research; a little analysis; throw in a little personal experience and some prayer. Whammo! A good book.

I was wrong.

Throughout the process of writing this book I have experienced what I would call an unending spiritual attack. I don't usually buy into what I call the *typical* Christian response when bad things happen: "Ahhh, *someone* doesn't want this to happen." I am the last person to say, "Satan is obviously against my doing this project." Those kinds of statements have always sounded like excuses to me, lines from someone who can't admit a failure.

My experience with this project has taught me otherwise. As I have brainstormed, written and edited *Dewitched*, my children have been sick. My wife and I have endured a stream of expensive breakdowns, including the transmission in our minivan and the furnace in our house. We have seen and felt an interesting assortment of "things" in our home. I'd call them spirits, but that may sound a little too dramatic. Once, in the middle of the night, my oldest daughter was covered with a blanket by something she says looked like an adult, while everyone else in the house slept. My youngest daughter has experienced night terrors causing her to run screaming from her room and leap into our bed.

In addition to these physical manifestations, there have been spiritual attacks. I have felt depressed most of the time; Our typically happy family has also felt a heavy spiritual depression.

I am not complaining about the opportunity I've had to write this book. Rather, I am telling you how I've felt so you can know how dangerous this subject is. Studying another belief system as powerful as Wicca and Satanism means opening yourself up to a world that will affect you. There is no "can affect you." These concepts *will* attempt to get under your skin and into your soul, and corrupt your relationship with God, your family, and your friends. There are no spiritual giants in spiritual warfare. No one is immune to attack.

That's why I want to pass on to you a few guidelines for how to approach this subject.

First, be careful. Pray. Read God's word. If I sound like a parent, I mean to sound that way. Your only defense against evil is to immerse yourself in God. So do that however you choose. My approach: I've spent hours praying for protection. Mostly for myself and my family. I have also prayed for you, yoo.

Second, read this book with another person. You are about to journey into a dangerous world. You wouldn't walk into a dark tunnel alone, would you? Satan's best weapon against us is to make us feel alone, like we're the only ones who are discovering. When he does this, he is able to tell us whatever he wants and we are likely to listen to and believe him. Find a friend, and read this book together.

Third, be aware that you are going to be frustrated as you read this book if you are not an evangelical Christian. I'm not downing you if you're *not* a Christian, but my opinion and analysis is clearly from the perspective of a believer.

A final word of direction: this book examines Satanism and

Witchcraft in two ways. First, there is an ongoing story about people struggling with unseen forces. I have tried to *show* you how some of the principles in this book are used and how they can affect the body of Christ. Second, each chapter contains facts about Witchcraft and Satanism. I have tried to give you the highlights with some depth, but have not explored every detail of the religions. There are scads of lengthy Internet sites and books available that delve into more detail than I give here.

The apostle Paul tells us that we don't wrestle against powers we can see, but against powers we can't see. We are like people boxing with shadows—always swinging but never knowing if we've landed an effective punch and never knowing when another punch will come at us. I hope this book helps you know what to look for and how to protect yourself. I hope this book helps you better understand what you are fighting.

Does it sound too trite to say, I'm praying for you? I hope not.

# 1800 DENVER STREET
## *The Old Religion*

$P$aul and Jared sat waiting for the girls outside Don's Quik-Stop under a moonless night. Kids gathered at Don's on the weekends, mostly because of the huge parking lot, cheap gas, microwavable burritos, and cold Pepsi. They hung out and snacked in the parking lot until something interesting happened. Don worked the weekend shift because he loved talking with the kids. If you talked to Don long enough, you could usually snag a free burrito.

Clarke City was the kind of place parents wished they had been raised and kids couldn't wait to escape. Downtown, the older section of the city, looked like a Norman Rockwell painting at Christmas. Old gas lanterns lined the streets, inviting you to window shop at a variety of old-time specialty stores. The light that reflected off the red brick streets told of a history long forgotten. On the outskirts of the city, trees lined the neighborhood sidewalks, where people welcomed each other like family. People held onto old values and even older money. In this comfortable atmosphere, the people of Clarke City believed the world was as comfortable as their own hometown.

Tonight was different. A cold dampness clung to the still night air making Clarke City feel like the inside of a coffin. The town felt uneasy and tense. Unlit gas lamps darkened downtown. Frustrated and quick-tempered drivers honked and yelled as they passed Don's.

Jared sat in the passenger seat of Paul's '99 Dodge Shadow, pushing an unusual combination of burritos and cheap snack-food into his thin face. His sandy blonde hair, skinny body, and quirky sense of humor made him a popular kid at Clarke City High. Last year, a lunch table full of cheerleaders voted him the funniest guy on campus.

"What did they say they wanted to do?" Paul asked Jared. Paul's deep voice sounded like a command from a drill sergeant. The interior lights bounced off his heavily gelled black hair as he sat behind the wheel, flipping through CDs looking for the perfect tunes for their Friday night. Paul was best known on campus for his leadership ability. He led last year's soccer team to the division championships. He often led the youth group of Clarke City Community Church in prayer or Scripture reading.

"I have no idea," Jared said, burrito juice running down the corners of his mouth.

"I left my other CD case at home. All of these are lame," Paul said as he reached for the button on the radio. Paul's car stereo was actually newer than the car. Nicer too.

*"The sheriff's office reports that there are still no suspects in the death of the cows at Salt Creek Farm, north of the city. A spokesman for the sheriff's department told KCBH news that the slaughter appeared to be some kind of ritualistic killing. Officials say it will be weeks before they can piece together the clues."*

"It's weird about all those cow-killings, huh? I heard they totally butchered the things." Jared said, fumbling through Paul's glove compartment looking for an old ketchup packet.

"I know," Paul said. "It's creepy to think that anyone you pass in town could be the killer! Shelby told me—"

*Thump, thump, thump.* The car shook. Paul and Jared jumped as a few expletives slipped out. Paul jumped out to confront whoever had dented his car, while Jared caught his breath.

Shelby stood at the bumper of Paul's car smiling. Shelby was a cute girl with the personality to match. Her deep blue eyes squinted as she laughed. Her long, curly red hair glowed like fire in the light of Don's neon sign and framed her pale, lightly freckled complexion.

"I hope I'm not interrupting a tender moment!" she joked.

"If you dented it, you're going to get hurt." Paul fumed, inspecting the damage.

"Oh, Paul. I would never want to do anything to hurt your baby."

"Whatever, it's nicer than your car," Paul said, pointing at the hand-me-down vehicle Shelby got from her brother last year when he left for college.

Mary, still sitting in Shelby's car, pulled her blonde hair back into a ponytail. Her makeup accentuated her high cheekbones, full lips, and chocolate-brown eyes. She embodied the all-American girl. Mary could have had a date each weekend, if her parents had let her.

"Were you listening to the radio just now? Did you hear they found another cow?" Paul asked, a little louder than usual, hoping Mary would hear too.

"We heard. It's creepy," Mary said, getting out of Shelby's car.

"Who would want to kill a cow? Sure, they're stupid and they reek, but they're harmless," Jared said as he got out of the car and joined the group.

"My dad says that they're part of a cult or something," Mary relayed.

"Yeah, and my dad has seen some of the murdered cows. He says it's really sick," Shelby quickly added.

Mary and Shelby's fathers had the inside track on the ritualistic cow killings in Clarke City. Shelby's dad was the pudgy police chief who cruised the parking lots at curfew, making sure all the kids were off the streets. He told Shelby some of the details of the killings, but it was Mary's dad who boldly passed along his theories. He was the youth pastor of Clarke City Community Church, the largest church in town. He was the kind of youth pastor who walked the lunchroom of the school, looking for someone to encourage or for a face he'd never met. Most of the kids in Clarke City liked Mary's dad, all of them were afraid of Shelby's.

"So, what's up. What do y'all want to do?" Paul couldn't stand a weekend without a schedule. Friday night was quickly slipping away. "Hey, I know! Let's check out the Denver Street house. They say that on nights like this, a mysterious light appears in the window." Paul's voice took on a spooky tone.

"Who are *they*," Mary asked, "and why would *they* care about *that* house?"

"Who knows," Jared quipped. "We may just find a group of witches dancing around," his voice lowered to a whisper, "*a golden calf!*" He let out an eerie laugh, causing the girls to let out a good-natured scream.

"My dad says that place is dangerous," Shelby said. Her adventurous attitude took a quick vacation. "He said that some of his officers won't even cruise Denver Street unless they have to."

"My dad would kill me if he knew I went near that house," Mary added.

"Come on," Paul said. "It's not like we're breaking the law or anything. I'm bored. The place is empty." Paul headed for the driver's seat of his car. In his mind, the plan was made. They were going.

Mary and Shelby looked at each other. "What if we go, but don't go *inside?*" Shelby said. "I'll ride along," Mary agreed, "but I'm not getting out of the car."

Paul drove quickly past beautiful houses with manicured lawns. Within minutes, they were driving through the old section of town. They passed closed factories and empty parking lots. Soon, they headed down an unlit street. Denver Street was in a mostly unoccupied part of the city. Years ago, the rich folks had nice houses here. Now, the neighborhoods north of the city were mostly empty and run-down. The abandoned houses and the garbage-lined streets made this part of Clarke City feel unsafe at any time of the day.

The house at 1800 Denver Street was legendary. It was a monument to teenage partying, a shelter for homeless people, and an inspiration for numerous ghost stories. Someone or something had broken the windows and kicked in the doors long ago. Drunken teens looking for a good time, spray painted foul words in gray and black on the sides of the house. It played tricks on your mind, teasing you into seeing ghosts and demons floating around, even if none was there.

The connection of the house to Satan worship started with Mary's dad. His youth group was exploring the evils of Witchcraft and the probability of witches practicing "right here in Clarke City." The kids rolled their eyes when he announced that the Denver Street house was a satanic place because the address, 1800, was the sum of three 600s. Take away the zeroes, and you were left with 666. According to Mary's dad, the connection to 666 proved that Satanists designed the house; therefore, it was pure evil. Although the kids were skeptical, this crazy idea added to the spookiness of the house.

Paul cruised to a stop outside the house. The kids got out, leaned against Paul's car, and stared at the property.

"There's no way I'm going in there. No way," Shelby said.

Mary joined Shelby. There was strength in numbers. "Me neither, Shel. I'm with you. We're staying. You guys go."

Paul got pushy. "Sheesh, we're here. Have a little adventure, why don't ya."

As the teenagers stood there, the house felt more dangerous than they could have imagined. It wasn't the way the house looked; rather, it was the way they felt.

Electricity surged through the air. The house appeared to be moving rhythmically, very lightly; up, then down; out, then in, like an old man taking long, deep breaths.

"Let's not just stand here." Paul wanted to get inside. He, Jared, and Shelby headed for the backyard.

"Shelby! What are you doing?" Mary asked.

Shelby turned to face Mary wearing a curious smile. "I give up. I'm curious. I wouldn't stand out here alone if I were you. You might as well come."

The backyard was just as intense as the front. A few old couches, empty beer cans, and fast food wrappers spread out over the yard. Obviously, this place had seen its share of parties. The shed wore spray-painted names of some of their friends: a couple who died in a car accident on prom night; a girl who passed away from cancer; and a few no one knew. It served as some kind of memorial.

Shelby's "whoa" broke the silence. "Guys, get over here." They saw it the second they turned to see where she was pointing. A candle was burning in the window.

"We have to go in now!" A lit candle in an abandoned house was bait for Paul.

Shelby tried keeping him outside for as long as she could. "Guys, think about it. If there's a candle burning, that probably means someone lives there. If someone lives there, they are not going to be thrilled that we're inside their house. I say we head for the . . ."

"Look at the back door!" Mary interrupted, almost shouting. She quickly held herself back for fear of drawing attention to the group.

The door was hanging open. It all started to add up to one creepy moment, the kind your dad invents for a spooky, late-night story on the family campout. An abandoned house, a trashed backyard, an open door, and a burning candle caused the hair to stand up on the backs of their necks.

As if they were being pulled, Paul and Jared walked toward the open door. Shelby walked slowly toward the door with Mary clutching her arm. They huddled together. A trace of warmth radiated from the handle of the old, worn door. Small shards of jagged glass glistened from the windowpanes in the door, which hung loosely on the hinges and creaked as Paul opened it.

As they slowly entered the house, the creepy feeling escalated. The smell of stale perfume hung heavily in the air. Yellowed paper peeled from the walls. In the far corner, the ceiling was falling in. The floor creaked underfoot. Outside was spooky. Inside was terrifying.

The group huddled together and moved slowly toward the room with the burning candle. Through the beat up kitchen, down the hall and past closed doors no one was brave enough to open, they inched along.

"Do you guys feel that?" Shelby asked. The house felt pressurized. The air in the house pushed against them. It felt like hands all over each of them, pushing hard against their bodies. The closer they got to the flickering light, the more pressure they felt.

Finally, they reached the room. The candle sat in the corner, on a table covered with a small cloth.

The candle gave enough light for them to see the strange markings in the room: symbols, stars, names. Words were written on the floor in another language. The pressure they'd been feeling escalated.

Mary was the first to speak up. "Okay, I've come inside. I've gone along with this long enough."

"Oh calm down," Paul said. "Hey Jared, wanna explore?" The guys headed out of the room, but not confidently. They crept along the dark hallways, unsure of which direction to head. Mary and Shelby stayed in the room and looked around. Shelby checked out the markings on the wall while Mary headed toward the table.

The candle stood like a guard standing watch as it cast its glow over several objects, including a small, metal disk with a pentagram on it, a wooden stick with some strange markings, and a few randomly placed pieces of paper. Mary picked up the stick, looked at it, and slipped it into her back pocket. Shelby didn't notice.

"Hey, Mary," Shelby said, motioning her over to where she stood. "This is gross. You have to see this."

On the floor was what appeared to be an animal's tail with a small piece of paper wrapped around it. "Pick it up!" Shelby dared.

"No way." Mary's voice shook. Shelby reached for the object and held it up so they could see it. Black, course fur covered the long, skinny tail. A clean cut marked the place where the tail was attached.

"Look at the dried blood on it. This isn't fresh," Shelby observed, like an amateur detective.

"Uhhh, no. It stinks! Definitely not fresh!" Mary said holding her nose.

"No," Shelby said, "that's not the smell of dead tail. That's cow poop. The thing smells like a farm."

"Hey girls!" Jared yelled, making Shelby drop the tail. "Come here. You've got to see this." The girls gladly left the room. They wanted to go home. The girls walked toward the sound of Jared's voice. The floor creaked under them.

"I can see through the crack in the door. Light is coming from the basement, but I can't get the door opened. There's someone living in the basement or using it for something," Paul said as he pushed against the door, trying to widen the opening.

Jared walked back to the room with the candle, blew it out and walked back to the basement door. "You know, I think the stairs lead down to a room directly under the one with the candle. When I blew out the candle, I could see light coming from underneath the floorboards."

As Jared was talking, the group heard a loud creak coming from another room. The sound sent the group running to the car. Paul had his keys in hand before he got to the car. He fired up the engine. Chests heaving, sweat running into their eyes, Mary and Shelby sat close together in the back seat.

"That was stupid!" Mary yelled, half crying, half laughing.

"What was that noise?" Jared asked. He was not laughing.

"It was nothing. I ran because all of you ran." Paul was determined to be the hero until the end, always acting confident, even when he was freaking out on the inside like he was then.

The group drove back to Don's. They would have something to

talk about Monday at school. By lunchtime, the entire student body would be talking about this.

⁂

THREE HOUSES DOWN, sitting on the steps of another abandoned house, a young girl watched the action unfold. The dark night and her black clothes made her nearly impossible to see. A few minutes ago, she was setting up for the meeting. Candles were lighted; magical tools, out and ready. Her altar was set up.

Now, she waited for the group to drive off Denver Street so she could get back and finish what she started. Hopefully, the group wouldn't come back. Hopefully, she wouldn't be interrupted again.

## DEWITCHING WITCHCRAFT

### GRASPING PRE-HISTORY

The history of Witchcraft and Satanism is muddy. The story lines originate during a time in history for which we have few specifics. Most witches will tell you that their story began when the first humans started walking upright, on two legs. They believe that it originated with ancient humanity.

We learn about ancient societies in one of two ways—either by reading what they wrote or by looking at the objects, such as the art, trash, or buildings, they left behind. By sifting through these artifacts,

9

scholars put together a semi-accurate understanding of what these people were like. In some cases, understanding them is as simple as reading a document they wrote. However, writing wasn't developed until around 3200 BC, and archaeologists claim that people walked the earth *long* before then. So we have to go back even further than the date of the invention of writing—way back. According to some archaeologists, and many Wiccans, we have to go back at least thirty thousand years.

In caves around the world, archaeologists have discovered drawings on walls which depict everyday activities such as hunting, planting, and social interaction. Presumed to be the artwork of ancient man, they appear to reflect their perspective on gods, magic, rituals, and worship, as well as tell the story of his work and life.

*Wiccans believe in the existence of an unnamed force that created the world. This force exists outside of humanity and nature, and is unconcerned with the world it created. Some ancient civilizations believed strongly enough in this force to base their religion and their way of life on it.*

## THE FIRST RELIGIONS

The story some archaeologists and anthropologists believe these paintings tell goes something like this.

The earliest humans roaming the earth were skilled in two areas: agriculture and hunting. Their skill in hunting meant that they would have plenty of meat to eat. Their skill in planting and harvesting meant that they would have a variety of vegetables to eat. Ancient mankind shared a close kinship with the earth. They had a mysterious understanding of nature. With no scientific explanation for how the world worked, they began to believe that there must be an unseen order or force that was operating their world.

Apparently, the first humans didn't have a name for this force, but they did believe it existed long before everything else and that it was the source for every created thing. It was invisible, yet it impacted the world. It stood beyond nature and would sometimes enter into nature for the benefit of humanity.

Ancient man's life depended on the meat gained from a successful hunt, so he wanted to get the best results possible. Imagine the time invested in hunting: he had to improve his skill, make sure his weapons worked, and wait for the right animals. Archaeologists believe that ancient man simulated the act of hunting, using paintings and clay animals, to move the spirits and magically influence the outcome. Cave drawings that depict animals being killed and small clay animals with holes in them give evidence of ancient man's rituals. The story goes that ancient man believed that these symbolic acts made him stronger and secured his victory.

This process of using cave paintings or figures is called Sympathetic Magic, and it became more and more popular as ancient man realized its benefits. Soon he became dependent on this kind of pre-hunting ritual, and it evolved into a regular practice that involved the entire community. Instead of simply poking holes in a painting or clay figure, one person from a clan would put on an animal fur and dance around while the rest of the clan would symbolically kill him with spears and clubs.

Eventually, a group of men became responsible for the regular practice and appropriate order of these rituals. As a result, these men became regarded as a kind of priestly class of ancient society. Some Wiccans consider these ancient shamans to be the first priests or religious leaders ever to walk the earth.

We know why they worshiped, and who led the worship. To understand *what* the ancient man worshiped, we have to go back to the cave walls and look again at the kind of artifacts ancient mankind left.

*Sympathetic Magic, the process of divining the unnamed creative force to work favors, is an essential cornerstone to Witchcraft. If intended for good, the force can benefit its manipulator. If intended for evil, it can be used against an enemy for revenge. Eventually, this becomes an important element in the use of Magic.*

## THE FIRST GODS

The kind of animals painted on the cave walls or made into clay figures tells an interesting tale about the kind of gods ancient man worshipped.

On the walls of some caves, horned animals are sometimes pictured with the hunted animals. These beings seem to preside over the hunts in some magical way. Anthropologists believe that these are the earliest paintings of humanity's understanding of god, a god that assured success in the hunt. Experts believe that this god was invoked and worshiped through ritualistic ceremony. Though many of the specifics about how ancient man worshiped are unclear, evidence suggests that he attempted to persuade the horned god through Sympathetic Magic.

We know that this horned god wasn't the only deity ancient societies worshiped. Agriculture was just as important as hunting, and apparently the ancients created a god for that too. They needed a god who would give them a huge harvest. They already had a male god for their hunts, and their rituals worked with that being. So they created a female goddess whom they believed ruled everything that had to do with the earth, including plantings and harvests. This goddess was thought of as the "mother of all things," who, like the god of the hunt, was persuaded through magical rituals and worship.

The mother goddess and the father god held everything in balance for ancient mankind. This mysterious understanding of the world seemed fairly logical. Because the ground gave life, as does a woman, people created a goddess who was in charge of the earth. On top of the ground, where animals and mankind dwelled, the male god reigned. This dual understanding of power is one of the most important seeds in Witchcraft: two gods working together for the health and security of mankind.

> *In addition to believing in an original force, Wiccans accept the mother/ father/animistic perspective of the world. Everything in Wicca flows from this worldview.*

## THE FIRST RELIGIOUS INFLUENCE

Most scholars, anthropologists, and archaeologists believe that the word *civilization* can't be used for any people group that lived before the invention of writing. While archaeology does reveal gatherings of people in many places around the world before the invention of writing, we can't know enough about their societies to call them civilizations. We don't know their history. We have no idea of their political structures, laws, or religious practices.

The first civilizations that used writing (and therefore have a recorded history) showed up in a land known as Mesopotamia, which means "the land between the waters." Mesopotamia sits between Egypt and the Persian Gulf, and encompasses some of the most important historical places of the Old Testament, including Ur and Haran—two places Abraham lived—Jerusalem, and Mt. Sinai. Most scholars agree that civilization began in this area. Archaeologists have also discovered clues about religious beliefs and practices that could connect to the ancient mother goddess/father god worship of the first humans.

Clearly, each society from this area borrowed part of its religious belief from another society. How did these religious ideas spread? Trade routes. Even today, trade routes make it possible for mankind to spread goods, language, culture, and religion.

The ancient Egyptians believed in a god of the Nile, as well as a god of the sun, a god of the agriculture, and even a god and goddesses that governed childbirth. This closely connects with the god-goddess worship, as well as the supposed animistic beliefs of the first humans.

Most Wiccans have long accepted the connection between the ancient cave paintings and the development of religious activity in Mesopotamia. They believed the Old Religion migrated into the religious practices of ancient Mesopotamia, which Margaret Murray described in detail in her book *Witch Cult in Western Europe*, published in 1921. Prior to Murray's work, few people made any serious attempt to connect modern Witchcraft with the Old Religion. Murray's explanation was accepted as close to fact until Margot Adler wrote in her book *Drawing Down the Moon* that Murray's story was a concoction.[1]

Unfortunately, there is no way we can know the answers to these questions. Some Wiccans acknowledge that some of their basic beliefs originated in the Old Religion. Others reject the idea. Many witches take pride in the mystery of their origins and, as a result, don't want the origins of their religion explained or examined.

Still, it's nearly impossible to ignore the connection between Wicca and the first religions to show up in ancient Mesopotamia. The idea of the female goddess connected to the earth; the male god connected to the hunt: it makes sense. When you look at the development of religious activity in the region where most biblical scholars say the first humans walked, the connection is impossible to ignore. Wicca is a religion that defies definition. It enjoys its mysterious heritage. Why? Is it because there is magical power in its mystery? Or is it because Wicca is more a construction of recent history and has no connection to any ancient history or teaching? We may never know the answers to these questions.

## THE DEVELOPMENT OF SATAN

Every society that has ever existed has had an explanation for evil. In some cultures there was a god who was the source of evil. In others, evil was the product of an angry god. From a human perspective, using manmade words and ideas, humanity has largely relied on a Satan type being to explain the nature and existence of evil. With the movement of the Old Religion into Mesopotamia and the plurality of gods within each religious system, ancient man mostly created evil gods who were responsible for every bad thing that happened.

> *A good example of an evil, angry god Marduk, found in the Enuma Elish. This ancient Babylonian creation story records an angry Marduk fighting with Tiamat. As these two fight, Marduk kills Tiamat, cuts her in half and uses half her body to create the earth, and the other half to create the sky. [2]*

We'll see in the next chapter that the idea of Satan—both the celebration of the humanness of mankind, or the worship of the demonic deity is a human construction based on the rejection of Biblical teaching. Where Wicca and Witchcraft claim development from the earliest humans, most Satanists base their philosophy, ritual and practice on a rejection of what scripture teaches about God, humanity, goodness and worship.

## DE-MYSTIFYING THE DEVELOPMENT OF GOD

The early development of Witchcraft (or the explanation of it) reflects humanity's search for the Almighty. Whether scholars are correct in the way they read cave paintings and clay figures, their explanation still tells us how humanity has been searching for a way to explain what they know is true. There is a God. He does exist. How do we explain him? How can we describe him? How does he interact with his creation? These questions have captivated us since the dawn of time. These are possibly the questions that fueled the development of the first religions.

The apostle Paul points out in Romans 1:18-20 that God has

revealed himself through his creation. Paul also writes that our hearts long for God when we stray from him.

Let's say for a moment that the Old Religion's understanding of God is correct. Wouldn't that match with Paul's words? Doesn't it make sense that humanity has a hunger for God, but often feeds this hunger the wrong way? Don't we often try to construct our own false gods either because we don't understand the ultimate God or we don't want to submit to him?

The Old Religion's idea of true worship falls apart when examined from a biblical understanding of God. Its confusing history is more a construction of modern thinking than of a piecing together of historically accurate evidence. It is inaccurate, and a lie.

On the other hand, the Old Religion does show us that humanity is on an urgent quest to find God. We will look for him everywhere. And when we can't find God, we will make up a god. We call him horned. We say he is male or sympathetic toward hunting. We do whatever we can to make God connect with humanity rather than construct a way for humanity to connect with God.

Mankind's search for God doesn't end with the story of the Old Religion. It doesn't end with cave paintings or the belief in the horned god. This Old Religion is believed to have migrated into every society. It is believed to have influenced the Romans, Greeks, and Egyptians.

In the next chapter, we will look at some of these movements and further discover how Wicca and Satanism demonstrate the need humanity has for God and the lengths we will go to discover him.

# STEPHANIE
## *The Interesting Lie*

$\int$ tephanie Patterson stood at the wooden podium in the packed gym of Clarke City High. Her T-shirt showed off her belly ring. If it weren't for her preoccupation with saving the earth and women's rights, Steph would have had guys lining up. Unfortunately, her attitude labeled her a tree-hugging, "man hater."

The principal allowed students time during assembly to speak about issues relevant to the student body. Steph usually snagged an opportunity to speak each month.

"We have to care about our planet. That begins with being conscious about how we deal with our trash. We need to recycle, but we can't stop there. We've got one planet, and we have to do what we can to protect it." Stephanie's voice cracked as she talked.

Most kids tuned her out. They nicknamed the blue recycling boxes "Steph Boxes." Worse, the boxes remained empty, a signal that the students largely ignored her encouragement to save the environment. Still, Stephanie never tired from championing her cause.

"Think about it. Each time you drop a little piece of paper, another tree gets cut down. All of this affects the environment. There is an energy and order to the universe. Recycling helps keep everything in balance."

Steph's sermon droned on and on. She pummeled the assembly with statistics about food waste and stories about poor, starving kids living right around the corner. Sitting there, listening to her emote, Jared couldn't help staring at Stephanie. He leaned over to Paul. "Dude," Jared said. "She is hot. Do you think I could get a date with her?" Jared pushed back the long strands of hair that had fallen into his eyes.

"No way! You couldn't land a date with her even if you were me. She hates men. . . . Oh, maybe she will go out with you," Paul joked.

"Shut up. I'm going to ask her out. I just have to find the right time."

"Listen, I sit next to her in physics next period. I'll ask her if she'd go out with you."

"No, no, no, no," Jared said quickly. "Invite her to youth group. That way I can slowly make my move."

Paul nodded his head. He doubted Steph would come, but he would do it for Jared.

⁂

MR. SPILLMAN'S NASAL, high-pitched voice irritated the students like the sound of fingernails on a chalkboard. The overly educated, sloppily dressed physics teacher flaunted his intelligence by using too many big words. Most students stared blankly ahead just trying to stay awake.

Stephanie sat at her desk drawing in a small journal. Paul leaned over. She saw him leaning, looked over, and punched him in the arm.

"Hey. How are ya?" she whispered.

"Good. What's that you're drawing?" Paul asked, pointing to the weird symbols she was doodling in her journal.

"Oh, just some things I want to remember," she replied.

"Is that shorthand? I didn't know you took notes in this class."

"No, this book is a record of my life," Stephanie explained. "These are just some thoughts and ideas I have."

"Oh, like ideas for saving the planet?" Paul grinned, turning on the charm. "I heard your speech today. You did a good job."

"Thanks!" Steph said, looking Paul in the eyes. Paul noticed how cute she was. Maybe if she turned Jared down, he'd ask her out.

"Hey, um, we get together at our church each week to hang out. Me and my friend Jared were wondering if you wanted to come sometime. We go to Clarke City Community Church."

"Uhhh, I don't think so. I'm not much into organized religion."

"Come on. It's just a building. You'll have a great time. There are skits and music. And free food. Besides, what else is there to do for fun in Clarke City?" Paul said it just like Mary's dad, Mitch, taught. Never take a no or a wishy-washy comeback as a final answer. Keep pushing until you get a yes. Even though this "evangelism" was aimed at getting Jared a date, it still counted.

"I guess, but I'm not committing to anything. Do you think I could bring some fliers about recycling at the school?"

"Sure. Meet us in the church parking lot just before seven. We'll walk in with you."

"Great."

Mr. Spillman looked at them and cleared his throat. "Do you have something to share with the class?" Paul and Steph shook their heads, mumbled, "No sir," and slumped down in their seats.

CLARKE CITY COMMUNITY Church stood next to three large subdivisions in the newer section of town. The church campus was large and on Sunday mornings the parking lot filled up early. The elders had hired Pastor Rick ten years ago to breathe life into the dying church. Rick worked tirelessly to make the church an effective tool in the community. Rick spoke often on community issues, such as homelessness and AIDS. He even delved into political issues, like the war on terror, and was a major force behind the Clarke City Clean Air Act that appeared on the previous year's election ballot.

One of Pastor Rick's major accomplishments was hiring Mitch McCorkle. Mitch worked relentlessly to make the church's youth program the hottest one in the city. His influence in the church extended beyond the youth ministry. Mitch used his marketing ability to put a new face on the stodgy, lukewarm church. He created the "C4" logo the church used on all of its promotions. Now, if asked, most members say they attend "C4."

Each week, over two hundred students piled into C4's youth room for ninety minutes of alternative music worship, gross-out games, and Bible study. Mitch called this RealWalk. Every Wednesday night, Mitch McCorkle delivered an in-your-face message and then served food.

Tonight, RealWalk seemed unusually loud and abnormally wild. The youth team upped the edginess of the skits, and the new guitar player increased the distortion on his guitar. The games were grosser than ever. Students bobbed for candy bars in a toilet bowl filled with yellow soda. Balloons were filled with curdled milk and tossed back and forth. After games and clean up, people settled into their seats and grabbed their Bibles from under their chairs. As Mitch stood to speak, you could hear the rustling of the Bible pages turning.

Mitch's fake mohawk haircut didn't match his wrinkled face and out-of-shape body. He looked the way any dad might if he wore semi-current clothes and smiled a lot. He tried a little too hard to be cool and fit in, but the kids liked him anyway. Mitch's easygoing manner and strong voice made him feel like a favorite uncle. He was easy to be around, like a best friend, only a lot older.

"Tonight, I want you to leave armed and ready to face the Enemy. We've covered the truth about Witchcraft over the past few weeks. Tonight, let's learn how we can defend ourselves." Mitch's easy talk and straightforward manner drew the students in.

"Witchcraft is all around us. Movies. Video Games. Television. I could tell you the names of ten musicians I know who cast spells and worship Satan. And we all know how evil Harry Potter is. We know this is dangerous stuff, but how do we protect ourselves against it? Open your Bibles to Ephesians, chapter 6, starting with verse 10. I want you to see something I saw yesterday."

All two hundred kids knew where to turn in their Bibles. They had read this a lot over the past few weeks. Mitch read the passage.

"Did you notice how Paul points out the battle we face? Not against flesh. Not against blood. Not against anything physical. This is an unseen battle, folks. Even though Paul mentions physical weapons, he's really using them as examples to help us understand spiritual, unseen weapons."

The message sounded as familiar as the passage. Each week, Mitch danced around the issue, using the same ideas and stories. But somehow, tonight, the message resonated with the students a little more. Maybe the increasing number of cow killings motivated the students to listen more closely.

"You fight this battle every day, and you might not even know it. I was talking the other day with Shelby's dad, Chief Collins. He said that there are an increasing number of strange things his officers are finding in the woods around Clarke City. Don't think that you are not involved in this battle. If you live in this city, you *are* involved, like it or not. I want you to learn a way you can defeat Satan. I've come up with a prayer you can pray when you are under a spiritual attack. I call it the Rescue Prayer. I'll say a phrase, and I want you to repeat it after me."

Mitch recited his prayer, pausing after each phrase for the kids to repeat it after him. "Jesus, protect my body, my emotions, and my soul from spiritual attack. Put angels around me, and give me strength to face the enemy. In Your name, Amen."

Mitch concluded RealWalk with his trademark, "You guys are awesome! Now go and change the world around you for Jesus!"

The band took their places, and the group began their closing song, a contemporary version of "Holy, Holy, Holy." Mitch walked offstage, and the teens exited the room.

"Stephanie!" Jared called, walking up with his hands in his pockets. "What did you think?"

"Oh, hey. Yeah, it was cool. I'm not feeling real well. I think it was those games. Had to leave part of the way through Mitch's thing. But it sounded good, though."

Outside the auditorium, youth workers handed out fliers to the RealWalk retreat. "Mitch is going to finish the series on Satanism and Witchcraft this weekend. Don't miss it," one of them said. Kids grabbed the fliers. One adult noticed that Steph was a first timer and handed her a RealWalk Bible, an inexpensive gift Bible with a homemade RealWalk sticker on the front.

"What's up with the whole rescue prayer thing?" Shelby asked Mary.

"Dad said it came to him in a dream one night. He said he dreamed that he was being chased through the woods and then he yelled out something like the prayer. When he did that, whatever was chasing him disappeared. He's pretty convinced the thing works."

"Weird!" Shelby said.

Mary nodded, a little embarrassed. Sometimes she just wished her dad was normal—normal job, normal clothes, normal hair.

"Hey, are you all going on the retreat?" Jared asked. Before anyone could answer, Mitch ran up.

"I need you four to help this weekend. I need Paul to lead devotions in the morning. Jared, I'll need you to help load the church vans. Shelby, can you and Mary make sure the ninth graders feel included? Great!"

Mitch sprinted off. The kids walked toward Paul's car, bummed over being told they had to get involved in the retreat. Of course, they would go. They didn't even mind helping out, but it would just be nice to be *asked* once in awhile, instead of always told.

"Anyone feel like disappointing Mitch?" Paul asked, frowning at Mary.

"I'm sorry, guys! I know he's pushy. At least you don't have to live with him. Try being his daughter!"

Stephanie jumped in. "You should meet my parents. They're really cool. My dad tells the stupidest jokes."

"Steph," Jared asked. "Why don't you come on the retreat? You'd have a great time."

"Yeah, sounds like you are all real excited to go," Steph said sarcastically.

"No, it really is a lot of fun. They're just in a bad mood tonight. Right, guys?" Jared shot a desperate look at Paul.

"Jared's right, Steph. It really is a lot of fun. You should come," Paul said.

"Well, I'm not sure. I'm kind of busy this weekend. I'll have to ask my parents. Listen, I'll catch you guys later. Thanks for inviting me tonight. See you at school," she called over her shoulder as she headed to her car.

Once Steph was out of earshot, Mary turned to the group and said, "Okay guys, who invited the witch's daughter to church tonight?"

Jared tightened his face as if he had just stepped on a nail. "Steph's mom is a witch? How do you know?"

"Everyone at school knows her mom does that stuff. How did you guys miss that? People talk about it all the time. I bet half the room tonight was freaked out by Stephanie being there."

"Heeeyyyy, Jared. Waayyy to gooo!!! Got a crush on a witch's daughter," Paul joked.

"At least girls like me," he retorted. "At least I got one to come to church with me tonight."

"Hey, I go out all the time. Anyway, I'm the one who asked her to come tonight," Paul jeered.

"She would have said yes quicker if I had asked her."

"Whatever. At least I don't have a crush on a witch."

"Witch's daughter," Mary corrected.

"Wouldn't your dad get a little freaked out that a witch's daughter was there tonight?" Shelby asked.

"Gosh. Hadn't thought about it like that. Yeah, he wouldn't be thrilled about it."

"Yeah, and he'd be pretty upset knowing that you talked to her, right?" Jared added, trying to get everyone's mind off his crush.

"It's probably best Mitch doesn't know about Steph. It'll save her an argument with her dad." Shelby said, putting her arm around Mary.

"Thanks Shel. Look, you guys" Mary began, "If anyone needed to hear the message tonight, it was Steph. Maybe God . . ."

Paul stopped Mary with another opportunity to jab at Jared. "Look you guys, if anyone needed an opportunity to date a witch, it's Jared. Give a guy a break."

Mary smacked Paul in the back of the head. They headed for home, talking about the evening, about Stephanie, and about her Mom.

## DEWITCHING WITCHCRAFT

The migration of the Old Religion isn't documented by any reliable ancient sources. There are no historical documents to read that report it. Since Wiccans trace their roots back to an Old Religion, but there isn't any direct historical tie between the Witchcraft that exists now and the Old Religion, we have to make some pretty big leaps to find the connection. We have to create a connection using some assumptions based on what sparse information we can find.

Some Wiccan scholars distance themselves from any connection to the Old Religion. They prefer to adhere to a mysterious understanding of their origins. Other Wiccans love the attachment to the Old Religion. Some Satanists might prefer to trace their roots back to the Old Religion, citing a connection with the earliest people who walked the earth and worshiped the darker side of humanity. Each adherent believes his own version of his religious history.

*In order to accept Witchcraft and Satanism as "true," you have to accept that their beliefs survived the migration of the Old Religion throughout centuries and dozens of civilizations. This "explanation" permits the vague history as to how Witchcraft and Satanism migrated from the Old Religion into a new belief system that spread throughout the world.*

The story of how humanity took the earliest of beliefs in the horned god and made it a religion that impacted all ancient cultures is an amazing mystery. Understanding how Witchcraft and Satanism work today means understanding how the Old Religion became the New Religion. Several significant and mysterious steps are important to know.

## MOVING THE OLD RELIGION

The best way to examine the spread of the Old Religion is to look at the early trade customs. As culture, language, and religion moved with people along the ancient trade routes, their religion also seeped in to each town along the way. With every trade, a new religious discussion took place. Each marriage of people from different cultures merged religions and new beliefs evolved. People began practicing rituals and acts of worship that reflected their beliefs, and eventually, these practices became traditions.

Belief and worship of the mother goddess or the hunting god evolved into a more defined religion that had its own stories, traditions, and explanations of how humanity was birthed from magical beginnings. The Old Religion acquired mythical creation and flood stories, temples and priests, and new converts.

When you remove God from the formation of religious belief, you have to follow these ancient trade routes to prove your point. Wiccans believe their Old Religion traveled a variety of trade routes leading to Greece, Rome, Egypt, Ireland, England, and, ultimately, the United States.

## THE OLD RELIGION AND WICCA

The two most important groups that use theories from the Old Religion and who mostly influence the modern Wiccan are the Celts and the Pagans.

> *The Old Religion pops up in Ancient Greek culture. The Greeks were well known for their polytheistic beliefs. Among the more interesting connection is their belief in "Daimonia" — spirits indifferent to the human world that could be persuaded through rituals.* [1]

### CELTS

The Celtic history can be traced back to approximately 700 BC. Celts are best known for their ironwork. Many scholars believe that the Celts' use of iron for such inventions as horseshoes, rims for wheels, chisels, files, and handsaws helped them migrate throughout the land north of Mesopotamia.[2]

Celts, much like most of ancient humanity, had a very primitive understanding of the universe. They believed in the mother goddess of the Old Religion and viewed the world as cyclical. They believed that the earth went through two key phases in each year: a dark phase and a light phase. For each of these phases one of the gods was in charge. During the light phase, or March through September, the mother goddess was in charge. During the dark phase, or September through March, the father god was in charge.

Using these two halves of the year, the Celts created something now known as the Wheel of the Year, which marks major agricultural points, including planting and harvesting seasons. They held festivals and celebrations at different points on the Wheel. One of these celebrations was called Samhain, which some people believe was the original Halloween.

This mysterious understanding of the year went deeper than the agricultural dependency and religious belief in two gods. The Celts believed that everything in the natural world connected to something in another parallel but unseen world. Humans had this same mystical connection to another realm.

The entire Celtic culture, including its religious practices, was held together by the Celtic priests called the Druids. Not much is known about these priests, except that they practiced their craft and led worship outside, in nature. Their temples were circles, often built among the trees. They had a hierarchy of priests, who were considered the wise men of their religion and who served as religious leaders, physicians, and scholars. Most Celts believed Druids could communicate with the dead, levitate, and change their shapes into animals and other people.

Today, the ancient Celtic religious practices exist mostly as celebrations of the tradition. Several of these Celtic traditions, including the Wheel of the Year and the major festival celebrations, have been passed on to Wicca. The priestly Druid idea continues to hold influence in many places around the world. We'll connect the dots between Wicca, the Celts, and the Druids in a later chapter.[3]

## PAGANS

Whereas Celts seem to be groups of people who were a society with rules, laws, and a religious system, the Pagans appear to be the exact opposite.

The name *Pagan* comes from the Latin word "pagani," which literally means "dweller of the country." Christianity spread throughout Europe, first to the cities, then slowly to the countryside. The history goes that the people who dwelled in the country were slow to accept Christianity, so the name pagan evolved from the word meaning "one who lives in the country" to meaning "non-Christian."

These country dwellers held strong animistic beliefs and practiced a variety of religious activities, including herbal healing and outdoor worship. The worship of these country dwellers was a mix of traditions some believe date back to the Old Religion. While we don't know much, we do know that their religion, which became known as Paganism, was generally earth based.

*In order for Wicca to have credibility, it reaches for a connection between the Old Religion, Celtic Religion, and Paganism. This creates a verifiable religious history that, in the end, gives Wiccans a credible religious history.*

## THE FATHER OF MODERN WITCHCRAFT

Many Wiccans agree that the most influential Wiccan that ever lived, and the single greatest human influence on modern Witchcraft, is Gerald Gardner. Gardner held a number of jobs throughout his life and always seemed to have an interest in the occult. It wasn't until 1938 that Gardner was officially a part of a coven in England. As Gardner got more involved in the coven, he began writing fictional accounts of witches. His most famous story, called "High Magic's Aid," was published in 1949. Later, he wrote a true account of Witchcraft called *Witchcraft Today*, which was published in 1954.

Borrowing heavily from the belief in the Old Religion, as well as other ancient traditions, and adding some of his own philosophy, Gardner jumpstarted and formulated the Wiccan belief system that we have today. Today, Wicca represents a variety of histories and beliefs, most of which were knitted together by Gardner. His efforts gave modern Wiccans both theory and religious ritual, giving Witchcraft the new life it needed. Since he revitalized it, Wicca has continued to grow.

## THE OLD RELIGION AND SATANISM

The Bible is clear on the identity of Satan as an actual being who rules hell and demonic forces. So it's not surprising that, since mankind walked the earth, many societies have worshiped Satan or the darker side of humanity.

> *When most Satanists try and establish historical evidence for their beliefs, they usually cite the worship of Set and other gods in Ancient Egypt, or they refer to Marduk and other Babylonian gods. When you read Satanic literature today (including histories, incantations and rituals) they often include these gods in some ceremonial or magical way.*

The development of Satan worship in the United States didn't really emerge until Aleister Crowley developed his own human-focused religion sometime in the early 1900s. Crowley was an unusual mix of sexual deviance, religious occultism, and humanism. Crowley was one of the most notable historical figures to use magic to attain some kind of physical results. He practiced a German form of sex magic, had at least one homosexual affair, and had many wives. Crowley believed a combination of ancient Babylonian and Egyptian occultism and was infamous for conjuring demons. Following a trance, Crowley penned the words, "Do what thou wilt shall be the whole of the law." The saying was the moral basis for his belief. His claim of a trance might be true, but his "great moral teaching" is really a rip-off from Old Testament teaching (Deuteronomy 6:5) and Jesus' teaching (Matthew 22:37-40). Crowley eventually died of a heroin addiction in 1947.

Aleister Crowley remains one of the few influential voices in modern Satanism. This could be because Crowley was involved in many popular anti-Christian practices. His influence extends outside Satanism and Wicca. Groups like the Freemasons and others include Crowley's teachings in their philosophy and history.

> *Some of Crowley's stranger accomplishments include writing homosexual poetry, and channeling a number of ancient spirits and demons.*

## THE CHURCH OF SATAN

Anton Szandor LaVey built on Crowley's beliefs in magic and the supremacy of the self. LaVey was actually an atheist and rejected the existence of any deity. "Satan" for LaVey was the idealized self. The perfect human person. According to LaVey's "Nine Satanic Statements," Satan represents indulgence, wisdom, kindness, vengeance, and responsibility. Because mankind is just another animal, Satan represents and promotes "sins" that lead to physical and emotional gratification.

LaVey started the religion in 1966 in his home in San Francisco. Most of LaVey's teachings and beliefs centered on the belief that man could, during his life on earth, become godlike. LaVey didn't believe in an afterlife and believed in celebrating the human side of our existence by indulging and feeding the senses. Regardless of the sensational images or the mythical tales that have circulated, the Church of Satan, founded by LaVey, claims they aren't the demon-conjuring folks who believe an actual Satan exists.

The satanic church was plagued with infighting during the later years of LaVey's life, and has dwindled as a result. Even so, LaVey, who died in 1997, remains one of the most influential members of the satanic church during the twentieth century.

## THE TEMPLE OF SET

The Church of Satan enjoyed a brief period of steady growth until the mid-seventies, when the church experienced differing views among its leadership. This rift eventually resulted in one of the church leaders, Michael Acquino, leaving the Church of Satan and taking with him several of the church leaders. In 1975 they formed the Temple of Set.

Unlike LaVey's organization, the Temple of Set traces its origins back to ancient Egypt. The name Set comes from the name of the Egyptian god of darkness. The belief in and worship of Set is really a lot like the worship of two gods at the same time (called duotheism, which we will talk about that in the next chapter). The Temple of Set worships the god Set as the real and original dark force (Christians would call this Satan) and as an actual being (as opposed to LaVey's atheistic worship of a general evil force). The Temple also worships humanity in a way that seeks the ultimate perfection of each individual. Their focus is humanity's attainment of "Xeper" (pronounced "kepher"), or human perfection.

The Temple of Set claims it is the preeminent satanic force in America today. Connection to Aleister Crowley, the teachings of LaVey, Egyptian occult practices, and satanic philosophy run deep through the Temple of Set.

*Today there are many organized satanic groups in America. Some agree with LaVey's teachings. Others agree with the Temple of Set. Others have created their own kind of belief based on their own satanic ideas. I've offered LaVey's ideas and the Temple of Set as representations of the organization of the Satanic Church, not as the only organized satanic belief in America.*

## THE INTERESTING CONNECTION

Neither Wiccans nor Satanists would say that they are connected in any way. Call a witch a Satanist and you'll likely get slapped. Tell a Satanist that they practice Wiccan Witchcraft and they'll tell you they don't hang out with weak-minded people like "white witches."

However, both traditions share an interesting connection through Aleister Crowley. Before Crowley's death, Gerald Gardner spent time with Crowley learning his beliefs. Crowley made Gardner an honorary member of one of his organizations. Although the two men weren't best friends, Gardner learned some of his occult beliefs from Crowley, and possibly incorporated them into his version of Wicca.

There is no evidence that Anton LaVey spent any time with Crowley. However, LaVey admits that it was Crowley's teachings that influenced many of his satanic beliefs. Aleister Crowley is one of many influential teachers in the lives of Gardner and LaVey, and forms an interesting connection between these two differing belief systems.

# Chapter 3

# DEAD COWS
## *God(s)*

*P*aul drove everyone to pick Steph up for the retreat, Shelby picked up the conversation where they had left off. "Paul, *why* did you invite her? There are some people who don't belong in church. Stephanie Patterson is one of them."

"Hey, do not even pin this on me. Jared is the one with the huge crush on her. I'm just the date agent."

Jared was embarrassed. Everyone knew how he felt about Stephanie. The time to duck and cover had arrived. "Date agent? You freak. I don't like her. I was just doing what Mitch told us to do by inviting people to church."

"Whatever! You like her, and I am the date agent. I set you two up. In fact, I should get a commission. You know, like the agents for football players. The quarterback signs the deal, and the agent gets the cash."

Shelby jumped in. "It's bad enough that she came to RealWalk. *Why* did you invite her to the retreat?"

Trying a different defense, Jared said, "I don't get what the big deal is. The girl is *hot*. Besides, when was the last time you invited someone to church?"

"Jared, her mom is a witch. She casts spells on people. She's freaky weird. I heard that Steph's mom always dresses in black and hardly ever leaves the house. This girl I talked to in chemistry class told me that they used to live next door to the Pattersons. She said that their dog was missing for the longest time and Stephanie's mom asked about the dog once and acted like she knew too much."

"Maybe she ate the dog. Maybe she tied it up by its ears, pulled its legs off, and watched it bleed to death," Jared said sarcastically, frustrated that they wouldn't get off the subject.

"Guys, my dad would freak out if he found out about Steph's mom. Can we just shut up about this before we get to the church?" Mary blurted out from the backseat.

Paul acted like he didn't hear Mary. "I wonder if she could cast a spell on her daughter so Jared can get a date out of this whole deal?"

"Shut up, Paul. I don't like her." Jared had had enough.

Mary's nervousness caused her voice to shake a little. "Guys, seriously. Don't say anything once we get to the church."

"Get used to this y'all. I asked. She's going. Looks like she's ready, too." Paul stopped outside Steph's house. Her cookie-cutter house was located in an upper-middle-class neighborhood. The nicely manicured lawns peppered with toys, revealed the family atmosphere of the neighborhood. SUVs filled with car seats and sports equipment sat in almost every driveway. Crime-watch signs hung on the telephone poles. Obviously quiet, steady, tax-paying people lived in this neighborhood. Certainly a witch wouldn't feel comfortable here.

As soon as the car came to a stop, Jared leapt from the seat and headed for the door.

"Thought you said you didn't like her," Paul teased.

"Freak," Jared fired back, already halfway down the walk to Steph's front door, where she was waiting.

Jared reached for her bags and loaded them into the car.

"Thanks for picking me up."

"There's room in the front seat with Jared and me," Paul said, giving Jared an "I am the date agent" look.

"Thanks, but I'll sit with the girls."

Steph climbed into the backseat. Mary moved to the middle. They all looked straight ahead as Paul pulled away from the curb. The music blared and no one spoke. Everyone, including Steph, could feel the tension.

THE PROBLEM WITH Clarke City was, there was just nothing to do. Burned-out factories lined the edge of town. Mom-and-pop shops peppered the center of the city, giving it that "stuck in the '50s" feel. Other than the double-screened dollar theater that usually caught B-movies, there was nothing to attract teenagers. So when promotion for the RealWalk retreat began, kids crawled out of the woodwork.

Kids began piling their sleeping bags and backpacks on the curb outside C4 as soon as school let out. Most kids were ready and waiting for the buses to arrive so they could find the perfect seat.

Jared and Paul stood at the curb, half-heartedly directing luggage as Mitch had instructed them to do: backpacks in one pile, sleeping bags in another. Mary, Shelby, and Steph worked inside, taking names and money and handing out the RealWalk Retreat Rules.

"So, Steph, have you ever been on a youth retreat before?" Mary tried to sound friendly.

"No, I'm not big into church stuff. What goes on at one of these things?"

"It's a lot of fun if you don't mind roughing it," Shelby responded.

"What do you mean?" Steph sounded suspicious.

"Well, we do get to stay in cabins, but the mattresses on the bunks are plastic. And we have to share a three-stall bathroom with twenty other girls."

"Plus my dad likes to do a lot of outdoor, back-to-nature stuff," Mary interjected.

"Sounds fun! I like nature." Steph sounded relieved.

A group of giggling, chattering ninth graders approached the registration table, excited about their first RealWalk retreat. The three girls turned their attention to the group.

※

AS THE BUSES rolled out of the church parking lot, blowing black exhaust, Paul scrunched down in his seat. Putting the earpiece into his ear, he tuned his pocket radio to the game.

"It's three minutes after the top of the hour and this is your local news. This just in: Police found another slain cow this afternoon in the woods outside Clarke City. There still are no leads as to who is behind these killings. Investigators are still on the scene. Local residents are encouraged to call the Clarke City police station with any information that would be helpful for the arrest and conviction of a suspect. Information leading to the capture of the responsible party will result in a five-hundred-dollar reward. Turning to national news, Congress roared back into session today with a series of debates on—"

"Paul, whatcha got there? Is that a radio? You know we aren't supposed to have those on the retreat!" The young, pimply-faced sophomore slipped into the seat next to Paul.

"Right, thanks," Paul replied, annoyed. He removed the earpiece and slipped it into his pocket. *Coulda stayed home. Coulda hung with the fam',* Paul thought to himself. *The things I do for Jared and Mitch. They'd be lost without me.*

## DEWITCHING WITCHCRAFT

### BEGINNINGS OF OLD RELIGION

Humans are interesting creatures. We have the chance to surrender our lives to a Loving Creator who knows us, and wants the best for us. Humans however choose to do everything they can to stay in control of their lives. Believing that we can do a better job and thinking that we're better equipped to handle our lives, we will ignore the existence of God. We will do our best to stay in control of ourselves and keep God on the outskirts of our lives.

However, as Pascal once noted, every person has a God-shaped vacuum. Wanting to stay in control of our lives and yet attempting to fill this vacuum, humans create all kinds of beliefs and gods that satisfy both their desire to be in control and fill the vacuum. They do this through an effective use of "isms." And then, they reach back into history—into the Old Religion. Into Celtic and Pagan beliefs. Into Egypt and Greece. They reach into every culture and tradition to support their pre-conceived belief about who or what God is. These "isms" are probably familiar to you. They define most of the ways humanity has tried to create a belief in god, while rejecting the True God.

### ATHEISM

This is the belief that God does not exist. Generally, atheists attach themselves to a more naturalistic worldview and believe that humans evolved from microorganisms.

DUOTHEISM

The Greek words *duo* and *theos* combine to make duotheism, which means a belief in two gods who are equal in power and authority.

POLYTHEISM

This is the belief that there are many gods who share equal power. Some of these gods get along; others don't.

ANIMISM

As discussed earlier, this is the idea that there are spirits in everything.

*Christians are* Monotheists *(this is our "ism"!). Monotheism is the belief that there is one God, adding "mono" (one) onto the Greek word "Theos" for God.*

All of these "isms" represent peoples belief in other gods. They succinctly describe some of the kinds of attempts humanity has made to replace God. When you look back at the Old Religion, you see these. When you look forward into Wicca and Satanism, these "isms" are blatant. How are they blatant? How do Wiccans combine all of these "isms" into their belief?

## THE DUOTHEISTIC STEW

From this basic understanding of the world and how it operates, Wiccans take their duotheistic ideas and morph them depending on their specific beliefs.

Some witches emphasize the femininity of the dual godhead, either because their coven may be all women, the group may have a special interest in fertility, or they may be reacting to Christianity's emphasis on God the Father.

Wiccans can be duotheistic and animistic. They may invoke the spirits through magic and ritual. Other times they may only respect the spirits. The same life force that gave birth to humans, and even to the male/female gods, also gave birth to the spirits that live in natural objects. This duotheistic and animistic belief aligns with the ancient Pagan and Celtic beliefs.

Some Wiccans are polytheistic and animistic. They believe in a powerful energy force rather than an overall creator, or creators, and they believe that there are gods in everything. Some of the gods are powerful, and all of them must be worshiped. Of these spirits, there aren't any that rise to the level of greatness over any of the other gods. Because spirits are in everything, Wiccans have a high regard for nature and the earth. These Wiccans may trace their tradition back to ancient Egypt or Greece, which were comfortably polytheistic cultures.

Many Wiccans are duotheistic, polytheistic, and animistic. They believe a mix of theories and traditions that support a long hierarchy of gods. Above all other gods, there is the life force. Just under that being, there is the mother/father pair of gods. Underneath them, having less power, are a myriad of gods; and at the bottom of the hierarchy are spirits that live in natural objects. Again, these Wiccans may draw their beliefs from more polytheistic cultures such as ancient Greece and Egypt.

> *The most unique thing about Wicca's perspective on god is their comfortable approach to who and what god is. They are comfortable with anyone believing what they want about their deities.*

Duotheism and polytheism permeate modern Witchcraft. We see this in their belief in magic, in their understanding of humanity, and even in their morality. It permeates their understanding of the universe and the afterlife.

Many Wiccan groups glean their concept of the god(s) from the Old Religion, but base their understanding of it (how it thinks, feels, reacts, operates) from very recent history (from Gerald Gardner's explanation, forward to today). Other Wiccan believers accept the Old Religion, yet they adhere to rituals holidays created by the Celts, thousands of years after (and completely unconnected to) the Old Religion. To access their god(s), wiccans use pentagrams (and other tools), completely unconnected to the Old Religion. In fact, the origin of many of their tools are most likely rooted more in Gerald Gardner and recent history.

A witches "pantheon" (their variety of gods) often consists of gods from Celtic, Pagan, Greek, Egyptian and other traditions. Each of these has different personalities and roles in society. Each of them often have conflicting roles and duties, making it impossible to know what their personalities are like.

The Ultimate Force, named by Wiccans to describe the existence of all things, lives outside time and space. It is largely unconcerned with the goings on of humans. Yet, this force is persuaded and manipulated through magic and ritual. Where do modern rituals come from? Certainly the Old Religion didn't pass them down to us. How do we know that this force doesn't exist to harm us? What if trying to contact the great unnamed spirit only makes it angrier?

With no way of knowing or supporting what their actual deities are like, Wiccans are left having to construct their beliefs and practices about their deities through relying on Celtic traditions, Pagan ideas and recent history. They're forced to reach into Ancient Egypt and Babylon in some cases. Anything to fill in the space between belief and practice. And, when they're at the end of their road and can't explain anything better, they rely on their explanation that all of this is a "mystery."

## SATANIC "ISMS"

In this area, Wicca and Satanism are similar in several ways. First, both Wicca and Satanism believe that the understanding of God as described in the Bible is limited, inaccurate, or completely wrong. Second, both groups completely reject the biblical definition of God. They either claim that God isn't as powerful as Christianity claims, or they claim that there are gods that are co-equal with God, or they say that Satan is ultimately more powerful than God.

*"Satan" means "adversary." While not stating it this succinctly, the Satanic Church in America has lived out this idea by taking a stand against the church on every issue.*

Satanists have been wrestling with the existence of Satan for centuries. Does he really exist? In what sense does Satan exist? Is he physical, or completely spiritual? Is he just a representation of the evil in society?

Usually, Satanists adhere to one of two most popular opinions. Either god is an actual being called "Satan" (or "Set," or possibly by another name) who lives in a place humans call Hell. Or, the god that is worshipped is the human spirit or the human race. "God" might also be the perfection that all humans are able to attain. "God" is the actualized self. The perfect human, or the perfection that all humans strive for.

However, Satanists also believe in a variety of deities that ought to be worshipped. If a Satanist adheres to a tradition that flows from ancient Egypt, they might worship Isis, Osiris, or Horus. If they have a belief that comes more from Babylonian occult practices, they might worship the god Marduk.

*Isis and Osiris were gods in the Egyptian Pantheon. They were the siblings of Set. The legend goes that Set killed Osiris, and cut him into fourteen pieces. Isis found all of Osiris' body (except the private parts, which she replaced by making them out of gold) and Osiris impregnated Isis. They named their child Horus.*

And, along with whatever gods the particular Satanist worships, there are a host of spirits and demons they might worship or pay homage to. Greater gods in control of different parts of the world. Lesser gods (often referred to as demons, though some Satanists believe differently about them than Christians). Like Wicca, they allow themselves to pick and choose whatever gods best fit their understanding of the universe.

A satanist would use a variety of words to describe their religious beliefs, including atheism, polytheism, or even monotheism (believing that the supreme god is either the human consciousness or a literal Satan-type being). Within Satanism one can worship only Satan, or Satan and other deities as well.

## MAKING SENSE OF SATANIC MONOTHEISM

Satanism, like Wicca, meanders around without any solid understanding of who God is. Because Satanists reject Christianity, they're left to construct a belief system beginning with who their deity is (unlike Wicca's, which at least attempts to reach back into early history).

The obvious difference between Wicca's and Satanism's perspectives on God is that Satanism is an honest acceptance of the biblical truth that an actual Satan exists. Satanists reject that God is all-powerful, omnipotent, or omni-present. While they reject the teaching in Scripture about God, many Satanists believe that their god is selfish and uncaring and that he or it can be manipulated to do harm or good.

A Satanist's belief that his god is selfish shapes his perspective of the world. Because their god seeks its best interests, Satanists must also seek their own interests first.

## MONOTHEISTIC TRUTH

Remember your Bible history? Early in the book of Exodus, we read the story of the Israelites' being held captive in Egypt. We read that the Israelites struggled with the polytheism that surrounded them in Egypt. Several passages suggest that Israel had opportunities (and sometimes took the opportunity) to practice polytheism. There were times when Israel believed that God was the only God, and other times when they decided to believe that there were other gods, some who were as powerful as the God of the Israelites.

The words in Deuteronomy 6:4 scream, "Hear O Israel, The Lord your God, the Lord is One!" This resounding claim drew the line in the sand for the Israelites. Either they had to acknowledge that God was one or they had to adopt the polytheism of the land where they lived.

Why is Monotheism so difficult to accept? Perhaps because Christian monotheism requires believers not only to believe God but to follow a strict moral code and give entirely of themselves. This self-lessness stands directly against the selfish perspective shared by Wicca and Satanism.

Monotheism requires surrender and selflessness. You have to believe that God wants your obedience in every area. This obedience begins with God's moral laws. Both Satanism's and Wicca's under-standings of morality (and of surrender and selflessness) stand dia-metrically opposed to Christianity. In the next chapter, we'll delve more into two very different understandings of what morality is.

# Chapter 4

# THE TAROT AND THE STICK

*Morality and the Rede*

*T*he loosely knit Saturday retreat schedule included a student-led, morning Bible study followed by an activity. Free time was scheduled for the afternoon, and students took full advantage of it. The retreat center had two swimming pools, a video game center, a snack shack, and volleyball, basketball, and tennis courts. Saturday afternoon on the RealWalk retreat was always the highlight of the weekend.

Jared and Paul competed in a spontaneous volleyball competition. Steph, Mary, and Shelby spent the afternoon in the cabin. Steph promised a tarot reading, and both Mary and Shelby nervously anticipated their reading.

Steph reached into her backpack covered with old "Linkin Park," "Greenpeace," and "Amnesty International" stickers. "Look, my mom taught me how to do this and I'm still learning. So, you've got to cut me some slack."

Sitting on the floor of the cabin, the girls joined hands. "Look at me," Steph directed. "Concentrate. Empty your minds of everything." Staring at each other, Shelby and Mary did their best to obey. This felt too weird. This wasn't the kind of thing you were supposed to do on a church retreat. Still, they had invited Steph and it would be rude not to act interested in stuff she was interested in.

Shelby broke the silence. "What are we supposed to concentrate on?"

"Hush. Just concentrate." This was Steph's first time doing the tarot on her own, and it was making her a little short tempered. "Mary, you're first." Steph looked at Mary's face while she shuffled the cards. Then, she began to slowly arrange nine cards in three sets of three on the cabin floor.

Shelby broke the silence again. She was nervous. This didn't feel right. "Cool pics! Is that one a picture of a girl arguing with an old man?"

Mary and Steph said in unison, "Shelby, hush!" Shelby's nervous curiosity made sitting still and keeping quiet feel impossible to Mary.

Each card Steph laid out was a miniature work of art, a small Picasso. "Each picture stands for something. Individually, the cards mean something. Together, they tell a story. I'm supposed to tell you the story the cards tell me."

Steph flipped over more cards. Mary noticed one of a couple clearly in love. She couldn't tell what the others were.

"Ohhhh, love. Mary, someone likes you. Yeeeaaahhh. The love card," Shelby tried to lighten the heaviness she felt in the room.

Steph's frustration boiled over. "Shut up, Shelby. This is the last time I'm going to tell you. It won't work if I can't concentrate."

Steph finished laying out the cards. She looked them over. Shelby was finally silent. Mary's eyes burned holes in Shelby, giving her a frightened we-need-to-get-out-of-here look.

Steph began, "Okay, this is what I see. There is a man. You love this man, but you're not sure he loves you . . ." Steph told Mary a story that sounded as familiar as an old pair of socks. "Do you know this man?"

Mary stared into Steph's eyes. In the few moments of silence, Mary felt as if she was looking into the face of an old soul, someone she'd known her whole life. The heaviness that hung in the air felt familiar. Time felt as if it had stopped.

Then, suddenly, a group of girls interrupted the silence in the cabin. They banged on the windows and pulled at the door, shouting to unlock and let them in. Steph quickly picked up the cards and hid them in her backpack while Shelby went to unlock the door. The girls rushed in. The room filled with chatter about who liked whom and plans for sneaking out after curfew. Steph, Shelby, and Mary left and decided to go watch Paul and Jared at the volleyball court.

Now that they weren't concentrating, Shelby could ask anything she wanted. "So if your mom is so good at this, why can't you do it? You said she showed you."

It was obvious by the tone in her voice that Shelby's pointedness seemed to make Steph angrier.

"I've only read once before with my mom's help. Besides, my mom and I are a little different in the way we believe. Tarot isn't as important to me as it is to her."

"So, if she's a witch, what are you?" Shelby asked, hoping to begin an evangelistic talk.

⁂

MITCH LOVED GROUP discussion. When he was not using the Bible to make a point, his devotionals were all discussion. Students often left feeling confused. The free-for-all format about an issue or theological principle was interesting, but nothing was ever resolved.

"Tonight, I'd like you to think deeply about your relationship with God. As you think, walk the campgrounds and find something that represents your relationship with God right now. Bring it back with you, and be prepared to talk about it. Be back in fifteen minutes."

Silently, the students spilled out of the room and branched out in different directions. Here and there they were kneeling, sitting, and leaning against trees. Some were praying. Others were digging in the ground or staring into bushes.

Mitch waited in the meeting room with his own object. Students began filing in slowly, silently, one at a time. Each of them carried an object. They gathered in a circle to share their object with the group. Everyone listened. Some people yawned.

Mitch went first. "I've picked up a rock because God is my rock. In the New Testament, Jesus calls Peter the Rock. The Greek word for Peter is *petros*, which means "rock." In that passage, Jesus is saying that Peter is a rock, the kind he can build a church on. I want to be that kind of rock for God."

"Who wants to go next?" Mitch asked.

Before the silence got too painful, Jared jumped in. " I brought back a leaf. This leaf is thin and flimsy. Sometimes my walk with God is like this. Weak, shallow, easy to crush. This represents my walk with God now. I wish it didn't."

A few more kids felt comfortable enough to share. One girl brought back a huge log. Another a pine cone. Each object told a story.

After everyone else shared, Steph cleared her throat and then spoke, "This stick reminds me of god, because it makes me think of power. Trees grow on their own through a power that we can't see. I think you can take the power that created the tree and use it to create other things like a stick cage for a bird or a fishing pole. I think if you give that power a name, you can call it god."

The students were surprised to hear Steph talk about God. They were sure she was an atheist. Some were even impressed with what she came up with. They had never thought of God in those terms before.

Mitch smiled encouragingly at Steph and thanked her for her input. Then he led the group in songs and read a passage of scripture about having a strong walk with God and standing up against Satan. He closed with a short encouragement to stand strong in the face of spiritual warfare. After his short devotional he had the students stand, cross arms, and hold hands. On the overhead flashed a copy of the Rescue Prayer. After reciting it as a group, they turned, uncrossed their arms, and chatted as they slowly drifted toward the cabins.

The walk back to the cabins always separated the kids into cliques. Guys timidly approached girls they liked and offered to walk them to their cabins. The "accidental" brush of hands created lots of squeals and giggles as girls recounted the incidents in the cabin bathrooms.

Mitch had asked Mary and her friends to stay behind to get things ready for worship in the morning. When Mitch wasn't looking, Mary slipped out and started to walk back to the cabin alone. Steph was waiting for her outside the assembly building, and they headed back to the cabin together.

Steph handed Mary the stick she talked about during the meeting. "Hey, you can have this. I made it yours."

"Wow, gee, thanks. A stick."

Mary's sarcasm made Steph respond emphatically. "No, look. I made it yours, see?"

The two stopped at the corner of the snack shack. Steph pulled Mary over to the picnic table directly under a light. As they sat on the bench, they were vaguely aware of the smell of musty wood and popcorn. Steph turned the stick over to show Mary the inscription.

Trying to be polite, but sounding less than enthused, Mary reached for the stick. "Neat. I guess I could screw a chain into the end of it and make it into a key ring. Thanks."

"Listen, I wasn't kidding about what I said tonight. Living things do have power in them. I carved your name in the stick because when you join yourself with the power in a living thing your power grows. You can do things other people can't."

"Like what?"

"Oohhh, fall in love, make someone like you . . ."

"Did your mom teach you that? Like with those cards earlier?"

"We're way past cards here. And this stuff I don't mess up. I've been doing this for years. My mom thinks I follow her religion, but I don't. My mom taught me about the power an object has, but she has no idea what can be done with that power. She's "spiritual" because her mom was. For me, it's all about power and controlling my circumstances. Look, I want you to see something." Steph reached into her backpack and pulled out a small package wrapped in brown, recycled paper. She passed it to Mary. "I keep a diary of my journey. Check it out. You'll see what I mean."

The flickering light didn't give enough light for Mary to get a good look inside the small, crudely made, leather-bound book. Steph kept talking while Mary's thoughts began to race. The book felt valuable. Each page of the thick book had something written on it. Some pages looked filled with poetry. Other pages were dated with strange looking writing. Things were pressed in between the pages. Hair. Leaves. A small baggie of fingernail clippings. Drawings. Mary thought to herself that the book seemed like more than a diary.

"Keep it for a few days," Steph said. "Look at it. You've told me about your spiritual journey. This book describes mine."

## DEWITCHING WITCHCRAFT

Talk about your crazy coincidences. We've seen that Wicca and Satanism are birthed from different worldviews. Neither belief system would claim any sort of connection to the other. In Chapter 2, we noted that Gerald Gardner and Anton LaVey perhaps knew and used the teachings of Aleister Crowley. Both men were clearly influenced by him. However, the LaVey-Crowley-Gardner connection gets even more interesting. They're connected another way, making the interesting (yet vehemently denied) connection between Witchcraft and Satanism stronger.

## WICCAN MORALITY

### THE WICCAN REDE

It's safe to assume that when Gerald Gardner went to meet with Aleister Crowley just before Crowley's death, Gardner wasn't expecting to gain some great moral truth. There was no way that Gardner thought Crowley, the poster child for satanic thought and blatant humanistic theories, could contribute anything to his Old Religion theories. Because Gardner rejected the whole satanic religion, he didn't really expect Crowley to offer him any unique, life-changing beliefs.

Even so, Gerald Gardner wanted some kind of moral truth he could pass on to other Wiccans, and sometime he must have heard Crowley's "Do what thou wilt shall be the whole of the law." This statement, penned by Crowley in the midst of a trance, became Wicca's new moral teaching. Gardner, wanting to keep with the amiable tone he thought was at the heart of Wicca, added a few words: *"An harm ye none, do what thou wilt."* Gardner called this the Wiccan Rede. (*Rede* means "counsel" or "advice.")

In a belief system designed to be morally ambiguous, the Rede is the *only* moral truth Wiccans hold to. The Wiccan Rede encapsulates all moral truth for those who practice Witchcraft. You're free to do whatever you want—no limits, no rules—as long as you don't hurt anyone else, including yourself.

> *Interestingly, even Wicca recognizes a need for some moral truth to be taught. Doesn't this demonstrate that humanity has an inner sense of right and wrong? The great struggle is possibly trying to defend where this sense of morality comes from.*

## THE RULE OF THREE

The Wiccan Rule of Three is simply this: whatever you do comes back to you three times more powerful. If you try to harm others, cast bad spells, or have bad thoughts, harm comes back to you, three times more powerful than the harm you dealt. If you do good things, that also comes back to you three times more powerful.

Here's how Wiccans say the Rule of Three works. Let's say I drive to the store, which is three blocks away from my house. On my way out to my car, the neighbor waves at me and, instead of saying "Hi!" I offer him an angry gesture with a response about how he better mow his lawn because he's making the entire neighborhood look awful. On my way to the store, someone in front of me is driving way too slow. I honk my horn. I yell out the window. I tail them until they eventually choose the other lane and get out of my way. At the store, I reach past an old lady for the last bag of chips before she can grab it. The cashier gives me too much change back, and I keep it. Upon returning home, I lay on the couch, ignore my family, watch television, and eat chips all afternoon. This example of a self-centered attitude creates a series of negative effects in the world. My neighbor will hate me. The driver in front of me may be ticked off at the world because it's full of crazy drivers. The old lady won't get the chips she really wanted. The cashier will get in trouble for having a short register. My family will be grumpy because I ignored them (although who would mind if a selfish person like that ignored them?).

Wiccans believe that my negative attitude and actions create a negative ripple throughout the world. My negativity makes others react negatively. According to the Rule of Three, this negative energy comes back to me three times more powerful.

The Rule of Three doesn't apply only to negative energy. It also teaches that my positive energy will come back to me. For example, I can give my neighbor a hug and be patient behind the other car. I can let the old lady have the chips and get pretzels instead. I can give back the extra change; and when I get home, I can share the pretzels with my family and then play basketball with them. Like the negative energy, the positive energy ripples too, creating more positive energy.

This idea of cause and effect can get more complicated than what I've described. How? Wiccans believe that the Rede and the Rule of Three apply to magic and ritual. Magic (when performed rightly) benefits rather than harms. So any spell that is intended to hurt someone is considered inappropriate by traditional Wiccans. Any spell cast to hurt someone will eventually come back to hurt the spell caster.

## THE CHURCH OF SATAN

Like Wicca, Satanism has its own set of rules and morality. In general, the basic satanic moral truth can be summed up in a phrase taken from a document by the church publication from the late 1960s. "If a man smite thee on one cheek, smash him on the other! Let no wrong go unredressed. Be as a lion in the path; be dangerous even in defeat."[1] This statement screams LaVey's humanistic, naturalistic philosophy: "Survival of the fittest. Do unto others worse than what they did to you."

It's not clear whether every Satanist believes this truth. Certainly there are adherents whose perspective on morality differs. LaVey didn't stop there, however. He created the following eleven satanic rules, which he said governed the conduct of believers and which are an interesting mix of occult beliefs and humanistic ideas:

1. Don't give opinions unless you're asked.

2. Don't tell your problems to others unless you're sure they want to hear them.

3. When you're in someone else's home, show them respect.

4. If someone in your home disrespects you, treat him cruelly.

5. Don't make sexual advances against someone unless they give you permission.

6. Don't take something that doesn't belong to you, unless the other person asks you to take it.

7. Acknowledge the power of magic in your life.

8. Do not complain about anything.

9. Do not harm little children.

10. Do not kill animals unless you're being attacked or for food.

11. When you're out walking around, don't bother anyone. If someone bothers you, ask him to stop. If they don't stop, destroy them.[2]

*Even Satanism accepts that humans, left on their own, need rules that guide their conduct. Could this be because without rules, we will ultimately destroy each other? Or could it be that humans have a sense of right and wrong placed in them from their Creator?*

These eleven statements may speak only to the group of believers who follow LaVey's teachings, but they represent how the satanic church has (and probably still does) attempted to assemble a moral system in the absence of the Ultimate Moral Law Giver.

These eleven statements contrast with Crowley's truth of "Do what thou wilt shall be the whole of the law." Crowley's statement represents his perspective on society: Get what's coming to you. Hurt others first. Do whatever you want, no matter who it hurts or how you get it. LaVey's eleven "moral" statements seem, at least, to encourage considering others.

When you consider LaVey's statements, they seem much more in line with Gardner's Rede. If you look at both Lavey's and Gerdner's moral truths you'll see that their morality is a lot alike. Both men claim to either have known or studied Crowley, yet their followers claim there isn't any connection between the two religions. Here again, their basic moral teaching, while anti-biblical and against the teachings of Christ, are clearly connected.

## ANALYZING MORALITY

We've seen that Christians certainly aren't the only group in history to have a list of moral laws. A little searching through history books would reveal that every society creates laws that govern and protect. Even ancient societies created laws, and some of them look very similar to many of the laws found in Exodus and Leviticus.

> *Other than the Ten Commandments, there were other collections of laws in Old Testament times. Some of these include* Laws of Eshnunna *(from Sumeria),* The Laws of Urnammu *(also from Sumeria), and* The Code of Hammurabi *(From Babylon). Hammurabi's laws are probably the most famous because in some cases those laws are identical to the Ten Commandments and other Old Testament laws.*

Even the recent history of Wicca and Satanism reveals that humans seem to have an inner need to be governed. *Why* do we need laws? *Where* does the idea of morality come from? *What* are the results of a life lived outside laws, rules and moral codes? If you remove God as a potential answer for those questions, you get very logical (and cold) answers. Why do we need laws? Because without them, we might kill each other. Where does morality come from? The constitution. What are the results of a life lived without obeying laws? Lawsuits. Arrest. Possibly jail.

But, when you include God as a potential answer to those questions, you get entirely different answers. Why do we need laws? Because they (in part) help re-establish the God-human relationship broken at the fall (check out Genesis 3:1-24). Where do moral laws come from? God knit them into us (check out Romans 1:18-32). What are the results of a disobedient life? Disconnected from God, ultimately an eternity separated from Him.

*Love* is the primary motivator for the laws found in the Bible. The God who created everything loves us. He wants the best for us. He gives us rules that shape how we treat Him (no idolatry, no blasphemy), others (don't kill, don't steal) and ourselves (don't covet, remember the Sabbath). He did this because he can't stand the barrier that sin creates.

Because he can't stand this barrier, God, in love, sent Jesus—the perfection of God's love for us. Jesus didn't just demonstrate the extent that God's love would go, he *told* us of the importance and power of love in our lives.

One of the teachers of the law came and heard them debating. Noticing that Jesus had given them a good answer, he asked him, "Of all the commandments, which one is the most important?"

"The most important one" answered Jesus, "its this: 'Hear, O Israel, the Lord our God, the Lord is one. Love the Lord your God with all your heart and with all your soul and with all your mind and with all your strength.' The second is this: 'Love your neighbor as yourself'. There is no commandment greater than these." Mark 12:28-31

Love is the motivator of God's commands. God's love for us birthed his laws. God's love in us is the motivating force to obey his commands and love ourselves and others. Without an understanding that love is behind God's laws, every law in the Bible looks like a tiny box every person is forced to live inside. Without love God's laws feel confining and strict. It's our belief in God, and our reliance on His love that make God's rules freeing.

*The love God has for us is unconditional. God loves us no matter what we've done! God expects that our love for others will imitate his unconditional love for us. This kind of love is absent from the Wiccan Rede, and goes against LaVey's Eleven Satanic Rules.*

# FRIENDSHIP?
## *Pentagrams and Baphomets*

*P*izza was the staple food at the McCorkle house on Thursday nights. That was non-negotiable. Because their week was usually packed with meetings, games, school events and last-minute church needs, Mitch's family pizza night turned out to be a good idea. Mary's mom ordered a large pepperoni-and-black-olive pizza with extra cheese and they would sit and talk about the happenings of the week but Mitch often stuck around for a few minutes only to disappear into his office with a couple slices of pizza to catch up on work.

Mary's dad spent lots of time in his home office. The walls were plastered with old retreat photos of kids with shaving cream in their hair, girls head to head grinning for the camera, the rededication campfire, and the like. On a bulletin board hung letters from kids thanking him for caring for them. Many repeated the same theme: He had been a father figure to them when they didn't have one. Stacks of game books and old Bible studies lay strewn across the floor. To the casual observer, this was the office of a dedicated and successful youth pastor. Upon closer scrutiny, it was completely devoid of any family pictures. Mary's third grade school picture featuring her new, self-inflicted haircut had been replaced by a youth group member's band picture. Her "World's Best Dad" plaster handprint from when she was five, had friendship bracelets and flea market finds stacked on top of it. There was nothing in the room to suggest that Mitch had a family. The youth group was his family.

If it weren't for the once-a-week pizza night, Mary wouldn't see her dad much at all. The only other time she saw him was when she hung out with the youth group. When she was with them, she was the center of his world. Mary's relationships with other students were more for her dad's attention than for friendship.

Because he was so wrapped up in his job and was looking for affirmation in it, Mitch often focused family conversations toward the youth group.

"The retreat was great. I think kids were impacted. I know that some of them were convinced to stay away from cults." His tone was confident, but his face searched theirs, looking for someone to agree with him and congratulate him for the accomplishment.

"That's wonderful, dear. You're really making a difference," said Mary's mom, the constantly supportive wife. She dropped her position as youth group sponsor last year to spend more time at home with Mary. It was short-lived, though. Mitch got a raise, and she decided to go back to school to finish her B.A. in psychology.

"The scavenger hunt was really great, Dad. How did you hide all of those things without us seeing you? The rotten eggs and the old moldy meat you hid were off the hook," Mary gushed.

"Pat Wilson did all of that for us before everyone else got there. Cool, huh?"

"And the Saturday night object hunt meant a lot to me. It helped me to see my relationship with God in a new way." Mary beamed at her dad hoping for his approval.

"Good, honey. I'm glad. You know that Steph girl seemed pretty nice. She really made an effort to fit in with the group. Her explanation of God was a little New Age-y, but after a few more weeks at

RealWalk, she'll come around. Maybe you should take her under your wing, Mare Bear. Set a good example for her, ya' know? She's got to be real careful, because that kind of thinking can lead you down the path of witchcraft. Satan will lure her in at the moment when she is most vulnerable."

Mary gulped her soda as Mitch began a rehashing of his teaching against cults and witchcraft. Finally, all preached out and full on pizza and affirmation, Mitch got up to head back to his office.

Almost as though she were thinking aloud, Mary said, "I guess I don't understand what's so wrong with other religions. I mean, I know they're wrong, but how? Why can't someone believe another way?"

Mitch quickly came back to the table. "Because God's Word says that he's the only way. God wouldn't tell us that if it weren't true."

"But dad, how do we know that our Bible is the one that's true? Isn't that kind of narrow-minded? Aren't there other ways of explaining or describing God? Like the way Steph said it?" Realizing that she should have kept her mouth shut, but having come too far, Mary tried to turn the conversation into a grown-up discussion. Maybe her dad would want to spend more time with her if he saw her as an intelligent, thinking adult.

"It's not narrow-minded if it's true," Mitch answered. He didn't like to be questioned. He saw questions as a personal attack on him. "These aren't questions you should even be asking, Mary!" His face turned red. "Haven't you been paying attention? The entire youth group understands what I'm teaching. They're all getting it, and my own daughter . . . ?" His voice ascended to a yell. Trying to gain control of himself, he said in a low, threatening tone, "Mary, don't be the one person who believes the whole New Age lie about religion. We're Christians. We believe differently. All of us."

"Dad, I'm not doubting. I'm just asking questions," Mary said, defensively. She suddenly felt as though her dad were going head-to-head with the leader of the local coven.

Looking at his daughter with disappointment, he said, "Asking questions is the beginning of doubt. You're on the wrong road, Mary. Go to your room and think about where you are headed."

At this point, nothing she could say would help her. Mary looked at her hands so that her father wouldn't see the tears and anger in her eyes. That would only make things worse. Mitch stormed into his office and slammed the door.

Mary turned her teary eyes to her mother. "Mom, why didn't you help? I wasn't saying that I believed in cults or other religions. I was just trying to keep him at the table by talking about this some more. You could have and stopped him." She sobbed, trying to control her voice.

Mary's mom had been standing at the sink listening and watching. Her hands clutched tightly to a dishcloth, knuckles white. "You know your father, Mary," she said with sympathy on her face. "He gets so worked up about this subject, but give him time. He'll cool off. Everything will be all right. I promise, Sweetie." She came over and patted Mary on the shoulder.

Mary headed to her room, alone in every way. She knew that her bleeding spirit would not be all right, even after her dad cooled off. Desperate to be valued and longing to be held, she laid on her bed, buried her head in a pillow and sobbed.

She didn't know how long she had slept, but when she awoke, the lights had been turned off and a blanket had been placed over her. Sitting up, she rubbed her eyes. She felt drained, but she didn't feel like sleeping anymore. When she switched on her bedside lamp, her eyes caught a glimpse of Steph's diary sticking out of her backpack.

Sitting on the end of her bed, flipping through the pages, she quickly passed pages of pentagrams and lists of herbs and spices. On one page she saw the English alphabet. Right next to it was a set of characters that Steph titled, "Ancient Runes." In a paragraph that Mary assumed she'd copied from a book, there was written:

*In the early years, we used this alphabet for secret communication. Using this coded alphabet ensured that the early crafters of our belief could send each other messages without being found out. Written in the right way, at the right time, these letters can connect tools with owners, making the energy and power exponentially stronger.*

Mary looked at the list of letters. They looked vaguely familiar. Suddenly, she remembered the stick she picked up at the house on Denver Street and the strange markings on it. She rushed to the dresser drawer where the stick was safely hidden. She studied the stick, noticing the strange markings that seemed to mean something. The markings on the stick looked something like . . .

ᚦTMᚲN

As Mary studied the symbols, she recognized that they looked similar to the ones on the page. Laying the stick next to the page, she slowly deciphered the symbols. Soon, the small word appeared.

ᚦTMᚲN became STEPH. Mary sat back stunned realizing that this stick belonged to Steph. How could this be? How did it get into the living room of the Denver Street House? What was Steph doing there?

A few pages later, Mary read about the spells Steph had cast. Steph had kept a detailed account of them, and the results. They made Mary's skin crawl.

March 4, 2001
Completion of spell cast three months ago.
Victim: Sarah Packard
Goal: Payback for lying about me
Result: Pneumonia. Hospitalized for a week.
Notes: None

July 23, 2002
Casting date of harm spell
Victim: Chad Busard
Goal: Stupid idiot. He will pay for it.
Result: TBA
Notes: The guys here in Clarke City will learn soon enough. Lie
about me and you will get hurt.

Steph's notes made Mary nervous. *Don't make this chick mad,* she thought. But what sent chills down her spine was the realization that she didn't know what ticked Steph off. If she broke her relationship with Steph, would hers be the next name added to the list?

Mary wasn't sure she wanted to stop hanging around Steph. After all, Steph was the only person in her life who didn't want something from her. It was nice to have someone who wanted to share things with her. For that reason alone, it was worth being her friend. Who knew? Maybe Steph made all of this up as a joke. Mary had been getting some good-natured ribbing because of her dad's latest series, anyway. It would be dumb to end a friendship over a little joke.

Toward the back of Steph's diary, Mary found several pages of poetry. Some of it was the normal kind of poetry a lot of people write. Some was just plain weird.

*For The Power*
Eternity in Summerland
To soar.
To walk the path beyond the pagans.
Beyond the old belief.
To a new way.
Stand strong
All hail
All hail the power that reaches into all belief.
All hail the power that gives power.

Mary closed the diary, and put it and the stick in her backpack. She lay in bed with the covers over her head, confused. She tried to imagine that she was the only person left in Clarke City. Safe. Secure. Comfortable. *What's more powerful? Religion or friendship?* Mary wondered. *How important is all this stuff? Does it really matter anyway?*

She drifted back to sleep. Down the hall, her dad was dreaming of his successful evangelistic efforts. Her mom was dreaming of Dr. Patterson, her abnormal psychology professor. Everything was peaceful.

## DEWITCHING WITCHCRAFT

Every religion creates or adopts symbols that represent their beliefs and the power they believe their religion holds. Christians, for example, adopted the cross as their symbol of Jesus' love and forgiveness because of the significance of his life and the sacrifice He made on the cross for our sins. In the days of the early church, Christians also used the fish symbol to identify themselves to other believers.

Like Christians, Wiccans and Satanists use symbols that represent their beliefs and the power they believe their religion holds. Interestingly enough, their symbols are similar. The main symbol in Witchcraft and Satanism is the Pentagram, though Satanists use the pentagram differently from Wiccans.

### THE HISTORY OF THE PENTAGRAM

There are many theories about the history of the pentagram. But, the truth is, no one can say with certainty where the pentagram comes from, or how it came into existence. Its origins are unknown. Some trace it back to early occultic religions. Others believe that the symbol comes from the pagans or the Celts. Still others regard it as a mystical gift from either Satan, or the Mother/Father gods.

Many groups have claimed the pentagram over the years. Different Wiccan traditions have claimed the pentagram for use in magical rituals. With each group the pentagram changes a little. They add symbols in the points of the star, they put circles and symbols around the edges of it. Through hundreds of years and traditions, the pentagram has been personalized in a variety of ways.

The only thing that doesn't change about the pentagram is the fact that it is a five pointed star. The pentagram can be oriented either with one point up or two points up.

Generally, though, most Wiccans and Satanists use a pentagram like the five-pointed star pictured below:

Wiccans typically use a pentagram with one point toward the sky. Satanists typically turn the single point of the pentagram down and the two points up. Satanists use the inverted pentagram differently from Wiccans.

## WICCA AND THE PENTAGRAM

Wiccans believe that four basic elements make up the world: earth, air, fire, and water. These elements make up everything important in the physical world. The idea of the elements comes from Greek philosophy that was prevalent around 400 BC[1] The pentagram is also connected to Wicca's animistic roots and the belief that spirits exist in everything. There were spirits of the earth, spirits of the air, spirits living in the water, and spirits living in fire.

The four elements are physical elements that have a connection to the spiritual world and the human world. Each element connects to a direction: the air is assigned to the East; the fire to the South; the water element to the West; and the earth element to the North. These directions are important in Wiccan ritual and magic. When Wiccans call on the elements, they are also calling on the corners of the earth, summoning *all* the powers of the earth and the elements. So, the pentagram encompasses everything in the world and every unseen force.

The entire group of the four elements is bound together by the human spirit. The witch brings the elements together to work magic and make things happen. Without the spirit of the witch, the corners, elements, and spirits behind the pentagram wouldn't come together. It's the will of the witch, the Wiccan's desire to create magic, and his belief in these worlds and the power of the pentagram that make the pentagram powerful. The following shows how all of this might look:

*Pentagrams and baphomets are used closely with magic and ritual.*

The Witch's pentagram is worn signifying the witch's belief in the elements, spirits, and corners and their power, and it is used in magic and ritual.

> *The power of the human spirit is an important element in Witchcraft. It has power over all the elements and symbolizes the Great Unnamed Spirit, which has power over all the elements. Wiccans believe that their connection to the Great Spirit assures they will one day be gods, ruling in another spirit realm.*

## SATANISM AND THE BAPHOMET

Like the pentagram, the history of the Baphomet is a mystery lost in time. There are different theories about when the Baphomet came into existence, and what the first Baphomet really was. Some believe that the original Baphomet was a human skull, worshipped by a group called the Knights Templars. Others believe that the first Baphomet was painted by Eliphas Levi, and published in a French occult book in 1924. The Levi Baphomet isn't a Pentagram at all. In fact, it's a picture of a full sized being, sitting down—part male, part female, part goat with wings and a torch coming out of its head. His picture is a few paragraphs below.

> *Eliphas Levi grew up attending Catholic schools, and was on his way to becoming a priest until he began studying various occult traditions and beliefs and was eventually kicked out of the church. Late in life, he made a living in France teaching the occult. He is credited with reviving an interest in the occult in France in the mid 1800's.[2]*

Other than the Levi Baphomet, the actual Baphomet that is used today in Satanism is actually Witchcraft's pentagram turned upside down. Most Satanists put the Goat Head from the Levi Baphomet inside the upside down pentagram used in Wicca to create an extremely strange looking symbol. *When* the pentagram was turned upside down is a mystery. *When* the goats head was placed in the center is *also* a mystery. The reason for turning the pentagram upside down is in keeping with Satanism's originality. Since the Wiccan pentagram is said to represent the more spiritual side of life, including the spiritual side if humanity, the Baphomet is upside down to represent humanity's non-spiritual, carnal side.

Depending on who you read, the name *baphomet* could mean a variety of things. It could mean "absorption into wisdom."[3] It could also be a Latin phrase rendered backward, which means, "the Father of the temple of peace among all men."[4]

Like the pentagram, the baphomet looks different depending on who is using it and what they're using it for. Centuries of occult tradition and occult books have produced pentagrams ranging from ones used as jewelry to ones created for satanic worship. Below is the Levi Baphomet, and two examples of the upside down pentagram with the goat head.

The Baphomet on the left is the Levi Baphomet. The interesting aspect of Levi's painting is the horns and hooves. Some believe that this is an attempt by Levi to include Old Religion ideas in his painting. The Baphomet in the middle (the star without the circle around it) shows the progression from the Levi painting into the upside down pentagram. The actual date for this progression is unknown, however this particular pentagram shows up in a French occult book published in 1931. The other version (the one on the right, with the circle) is the most common version Satanists use today. The history and development of the Baphomet is long and interesting. Even today, the Baphomet is changed often to suit the practices of certain Satanic and occultic groups.

This symbol has been the focus of many theories. The goat head in the Baphomet (either the Levi painting, or in the upside down pentagram) is said to be a variety of things. It could be a goat demon or a stylized version of another kind of god. It could also be the head of the Goat of Mendes, which is an ancient Egyptian god whose name means "the hidden one, he who abides in all things, the soul of all phenomena."[5] Obviously, the goat face, including the horns and the hooves could be a representation of the Horned God from the Old Religion. These interpretations of the Baphomet create another interesting connection between Satanism and Wicca. It could possibly be another place where these two "different" religions show a connection. Even though the Satanic Baphomet is the Wiccan inverted pentagram, both groups still use a pentagram. Even though Satanism claims to reject Wiccan beliefs, the horned god shows up in their Baphomet.

> *When he was the leader of a German sex cult, Aleister Crowley took on the name baphomet.*

The Baphomet is also thought to be a symbol of power (similar to the pentagram in Wicca), and its worn as such. The Baphomet is used in Black Magic for casting spells and summoning demons, although how it is used in those ceremonies depends on the person using it. It can be used in much the same way as the pentagram is in ritual and spell casting in Wicca. It can be used just as a point of focus in ceremonies. Sometimes, there are other symbols used in conjunction with the Baphomet. These symbols are also thought to bring power to the person using them as well as to aid in casting spells. Some of these symbols show up in satanic spell casting books like the Necronomicon.

## THE PENTAGRAM, THE BAPHOMET, AND THE CROSS

As I said at the beginning of this chapter, people adopt religious icons to symbolize certain significant beliefs. In Wicca and Satanism, the symbols represent power, a rejection of other people's beliefs, or a deep understanding of the inner workings of the universe.

The pentagram and the baphomet sharply contrast with the cross. Consider these examples:

### ORIGINS

Of the three symbols, only the origins of the cross are known. We know that it was used during the time of Christ, and after, by the Romans to humiliate and cause serious pain while on the way to death. We know that Jesus suffered humiliation, pain, and death on the cross. We can point to the historical existence of Jesus and the historical use of the cross. The pentagram and the baphomet have a muddy history and unclear roots.

### MAGICAL POWERS

The symbols of Witchcraft and Satanism do have magical powers. They connect to another realm. They gather forces for the express purpose of creating magic. The cross does not serve that purpose. Christians certainly use the cross as a focal point in their worship, but they do not call the corners of the cross for the poor, and they don't manipulate the elements, spirits, or forces with the cross.

### ANIMISM

This sounds similar to the previous difference, but it's important to point this out separately. Wiccans use the pentagram to connect with the spirits that they believe exist in everything. Christians do not use the cross to connect with spirits, nor do they believe it can be used for this purpose. Outside of God, there are no additional spirits to be appeased or called on.

Christians adopt the cross as the symbol of their faith because of Christ's death on the cross and what we believe about Jesus. Had Jesus been just an ordinary man or a good teacher, the cross would not be a significant symbol. However, because Christians believe that Jesus was God in the flesh, his death makes the cross a significant symbol. In the time when Jesus was crucified, the cross was an especially cruel death sentence. The worst times in life were often compared with crucifixion. In Galatians 3:3, Paul remarks that being crucified humiliating as well as painful. Jesus' death, while sufficient for our sins, was also an embarrassing moment in his life.

Throughout history the cross has been the most important symbol for Christians. We don't believe the cross has any special power. Different parts of the cross don't represent different powers. We don't believe that the cross has power in the same way that Wiccans believe the pentagram has power. We believe in the powerful act that Jesus did on the cross, saving us from our sins by offering himself as a sacrifice in our place.

The Christian symbol of the cross differs from Wiccan and satanic symbols because it represents a calling for Christian believers, a calling to a new way of life. In Romans 6:6, Paul comments that our old self—our identity before we believed in Jesus—is crucified (literally, killed) for God. As a result, we can live for him. Believers are called to share in the crucifixion Jesus experienced (Galatians 2:20), and Jesus himself calls us to carry our cross (Matthew 16:24).

These point to a different use of our symbol. It not only represents our Savior's death for us, but also represents our death and the resurrection of our new selves in Jesus. It represents our surrender. It represents the contrast between our old life and our new one.

Pentagrams and Baphomets are key ingredients in Witchcraft. Without them its impossible to accomplish any magical purpose, and the person casting the spell won't accomplish what they're attempting. It's important to remember the connection that these symbols have to Witchcraft as you read about it in the next chapter.

# Chapter 6

# TALKING TO DEAD PEOPLE
## *Magick*

*T*he guy who answered the door didn't look like the husband of a witch. His enthusiastic "Come on in!" caught Mary off guard. She expected Steph's parents to be at least a little freaky. His warm smile, neat appearance, and calm demeanor made him appear more like an old friend. Mary instantly felt at home.

*Seven steps inside,* Mary thought. *My dad would freak out if he knew I was this deep in the 'enemy's territory.'*

Steph's mom sat on the red-tapestry couch. Next to her were two other girls that Mary recognized from school. They didn't attempt eye contact as Steph's mom stood to give Mary a hug.

"Hi Mary! I'm Janet, Steph's mom. Stephanie has told me all about you. You feel free to call me mom. We're not much on formalities around here." Her shoulder-length blonde hair, thin frame, and meticulous makeup put Mary instantly at ease. Janet sat back down and patted the open seat next to her. Mary sat down. She could easily have been sitting next to her own mother.

"I love your living room. You've got a nice house," said Mary.

"Thanks. I've decorated according to feng shui. Everything is precisely arranged in order to bring peace and harmony to the home."

Janet told Mary about decorative patterns and the significance of color choices and the good or bad energy each bring into the home.

Janet's knowledge fascinated Mary. She had never thought about how to decorate before, but this room was comfortable.

"Hey, Mary," Janet suddenly said. "Steph told me that she messed up your reading on the retreat. I'd like the chance to do the job right. The girls won't miss you. Promise."

Janet led Mary into the kitchen, to a round oak table where Mary settled into the hard wooden chair. *What's worse than being in Steph's house?* Mary thought. *Having my future read by a witch.*

"Let's just sit here for a few minutes," Janet said as she looked into Mary's eyes. "Concentrate, Mary. I'm going to read your future, so I want you to concentrate on what you'd like to see happen to you after high school."

Mary was too worried about what was happening to concentrate, yet too curious to sprint from the table. Life after high school? She was convinced she wouldn't live past tomorrow if her dad found out what she was doing tonight.

Janet began laying the cards into nine piles. Each card told a story, and only Janet could decipher what that story was.

"This is good. See this card right here?" Steph's mom pointed to a card of a woman wearing a robe, holding a basket full of food. "This card tells me that you will have a good, long life. You'll be happy and successful. Sometimes I get another card that tells me the person will suffer. Good news . . . no suffering!"

The next card was a picture of a man standing alone in a field. He looked confused, maybe a little angry. Mary stared at the card and thought how much it looked like her dad.

"It's your dad, isn't it? This card tells me about your relationship with your dad. He doesn't seem concerned, or maybe he is more concerned about others than he is about you. This is the frustrating part about the tarot. It sometimes doesn't tell you everything. The frustration you feel about your father is a path that is not yet fully realized. As you are on a path, your dad is also on a path. What he decides, how he chooses to live will change your path. This card tells me that your future with your dad is uncertain."

The news was too real for Mary. Outside of Paul, Jared, and Shelby, no one knew about her struggles with her dad. Steph's mom was either a good guesser, or this stuff was real.

Janet continued. She turned over a card telling about Mary's love life, and one about the kind of college she would attend. It all seemed jumbled together. Mary focused on the part about her dad.

More cards. More interpretations. Steph's mom seemed to know everything about Mary. More than anyone could know, even her parents. Janet looked at Mary.

"There. How do you feel?"

*How do I feel?* Mary thought. *Confused? Definitely*! But what scared her was that she didn't feel *scared*. She no longer felt the urge to sprint from the table. She felt so comfortable around Janet that she knew she needed to get out of there.

"I feel ready to get back to the other girls," Mary said. It was all she could think to say. Her eyes darted from the floor to Janet's face and back to the floor again, not sure what to do next. Could she just get up and leave? Was there supposed to be a prayer ceremony? Was she supposed to pay her? Half expecting Janet to levitate to her feet, Mary cautiously looked up.

"You know Mary, if you ever have any questions about what we believe, you can always ask. What we do isn't any secret." Janet's calm, smooth voice made Mary wish that she was as sure about her beliefs. She had never been comfortable talking to strangers about Christ. She could tell that Janet was about to launch into a full-court press about her beliefs when the phone interrupted their conversation. She picked up the cordless phone on the wall behind her.

"Hello? Oh, hi! Yes, she called earlier and we're all set. We're meeting at Potts. Got it. Thanks Rick. Yes, I'll pass it on. See you then."

Before she had a chance to hear any more, Mary quickly headed back to the living room. Shelby had arrived and was stuffing her face with popcorn.

⁂

LATER THAT NIGHT, Mary laid next to Steph, bloated from too much popcorn and Coke. All of the typical late-night talk was over, and people seemed to be drifting off to sleep. Mary thought about how different Steph was. It was nice to be around someone who was not judgmental. Mary could say or do anything and Steph never tried to condemn or correct her. She knew her dad would be furious about her friendship with Steph if he knew what she believed.

Steph rolled over and elbowed Mary. "Hey, did you remember to bring my book?"

"Yeah, I brought it with me." Mary headed over to her backpack and grabbed Steph's diary and the stick she found on Denver street. Handing her the diary she asked, "So what is this book anyway? It's not like any diary I've ever seen."

"It's my book of shadows," Steph whispered. "It's a religious thing, but it's also very personal. Every witch has one, but no two are alike. You write things in it to help you remember the things you need in order to practice your religion. It's kinda like your Bible, except this is my own personal book. To me. For me. By me."

"Uh huh," Mary responded not knowing what else to say. "And what's the deal with this stick?"

"Hey, where did you find that? I've been looking all over for it."

"So, this *is yours*. I saw the marks on it, and found the code thing in your book. I kind of put two and two together."

"Yep, that's mine! Pretty cute, checkin' my name and all."

"So the stick you made for me on the retreat and this stick are the same thing? This is what you use to make things happen?"

"Not all the time. I use them mostly when I'm practicing with my mom, and sometimes when I'm casting and need my tools."

"Your tools? So this is like a screwdriver?" Mary asked.

"Not really," Steph explained. "Think of it as a magnet. I use it to draw energy in so I can make things happen. I can make guys fall in love with me. I can get teachers to give me good grades. Last year, I used it to get back at a guy who said he made out with me on a date."

"What did you do to him?"

"Let's just say walking isn't an option for him anymore. And it's called a wand, by the way. A magic wand."

Mary instantly knew that Steph was talking about Bobby Jackson. He was known for being one of the best players on the soccer team. He was also known for the weird accident that left him paralyzed. "You did that?"

"Yep. It's the part of magic we don't talk about much. When someone hurts me, I usually get them back. And the great thing is, they never know it."

Just then, Mary noticed Shelby stir and get up. "Are you okay, Shel?"

"Yeah. Gotta go to the bathroom. Be right back."

Mary watched Shelby leave the room. "Do you think she heard us? She's probably freaking out right now if she did."

"I've talked to Shelby some about all of this. She seemed to understand a lot more than I thought she would."

"Really? Shelby?"

"Yup. We've been getting together every so often. You'd be surprised."

⁂

SHELBY TIPTOED OUT to the back porch. Her bare feet froze against the rough cement slab. She almost leapt onto the wicker chair. Cell phone in hand, she dialed Paul's number.

PAUL AND JARED had planned all week to rent movies Friday night. Coke cans, popcorn, and chips littered the coffee table in Paul's living room. The lights were off, the surround sound was on, and the volume was turned up. Engines raced, the music got louder and more frantic. . . . Paul's phone rang.

"Hey, is that your cell phone? Who is calling you at 1:00 in the morning?"

Paul looked at the caller I.D. "Dude, it's Shel. I bet she's freaking out over at the witch's house." He put the phone to his ear, "Sup, Shel?"

"Paul, listen. What are you doing tomorrow night? I overheard Stephanie's mom talking about something at Potts tomorrow night. I don't know what's happening. Maybe a séance? It's worth checking out. What do you think?"

Jared watched Paul "chat" with Shelby. Long silences followed an occasional, "Uh huh," or "Really?" Finally Paul said, "Count me in."

Turning to Jared, Paul asked, "Dude, what are you doing tomorrow night? You busy?"

"Nah. What's going on?"

"We're staking out some kind of ceremony Shelby overheard Steph's mom talking about."

"Cool. A ceremony," Jared said. "I'm in."

THE SLUMBER PARTY broke up around 11:00 the next morning, but Mary left around 9:00. She was actually glad that her dad was picking her up to help him shop for C4's Fall Fest. She was afraid that Shelby heard her conversation with Steph last night and she dreaded the confrontation. Waving good-bye, Mary ran down the sidewalk and slid into the front seat of her father's waiting car.

"Good morning, Mare Bear! Did you sleep well?" Mitch felt guilty for losing his temper the other night.

"Morning." Mary was still a little gun-shy around her dad.

"How was the party? Did you have a good time?"

"Mm-hm," Mary responded nonchalantly.

Frustrated at not getting better responses, Mitch went into "dad mode." "You didn't get into anything you shouldn't have did you? No 'R' rated movies? No boys? No drinking or drugs?"

"No, Dad, nothing like that," Mary answered honestly.

Mitch knew that he had blown it. Mary just needed a little more time to get over it, Mitch reasoned. They drove the rest of the way in silence.

⁂

AS THE PARTY was breaking up, Steph pulled Shelby aside. "Hey, what are you doing for the rest of the day?"

"Not much. I've got a date later tonight, though."

"Do you want to catch a matinee? That way you can get home in time for your date."

Driving across Clarke City, Shelby and Steph headed to the movies. Steph sat behind the wheel of her car. Stereo low. Windows up. The car smelled new, mixed with a hint of patchouli.

Shelby started asking Steph questions about her beliefs. "Last night, I overheard you and Mary talking. You really believe that stuff?"

"Yeah, I learned the basics from my mom, but it wasn't enough. What my mom taught me only made me more interested. So I began my own journey for more knowledge."

"I know what you mean. My parents have always taken me to church where I learned all about the stories in the Bible. But there always seemed to be something missing," Shelby admitted, "until Mitch came along. He said that I needed to try having a personal relationship with Jesus. I tried, but then I saw how he ignores Mary until he needs something from her. It didn't seem like a personal relationship with Christ made much of a difference with him."

"Yeah, it's almost like their religious beliefs are more a part of their routine than something they really believe," Steph said sympathetically. "My parents have been going to gatherings since I was a baby, but it seems more like their club than their beliefs."

"Exactly. My mom goes through the motions. That's about it."

"Yeah. It's like, for us, this needs to be real. But for them, it's all ceremony."

They rode in silence for a while, each girl thought about how removed they were from their parents' religion.

Steph was the first to break the silence. "You know, Shelby, I get together with a group of girls every so often, and we talk about our spiritual lives. I think you'd fit right in with our group."

Shelby looked straight ahead, watching the road rise ahead of them, not sure how to respond. As they rounded the corner, kids were standing outside the movies, waiting to get their tickets. Shelby knew what Steph was asking her. She also knew that her parents would freak if they found out about Steph's practices. The thought of hanging out with witches scared her. But Steph wasn't too bad.

Before Shelby could say anything, Steph continued. "Look, I'm not asking you to give up your church. Hey, I've been to your church. It's a great place. We believe just like you do. We worship one god. We believe in living right. We study together. We even witness. Really, you'd fit right in."

Not knowing how to get out of it, Shelby said, "I don't know. I'll think about it."

Steph found a parking spot, and the girls headed toward the line to get their tickets. The cool, fall air felt good on Shelby's face. She was really starting to like Steph. She wondered if the other girls in Steph's group were anything like her.

### DEWITCHING WITCHCRAFT

"Magic is the ability to make something happen that you want to happen."[1] This was the perspective of the ancient humans as they sought to use magic to guarantee them success in hunting. This was their perspective as they worshiped the mother goddess through community ritual. The Celts and Pagans also had this perspective, that they could use physical objects to control spiritual forces and make something happen in the physical world that typically would not happen.

The use of objects, the human will and spirit, and ritual are the heart of magic and Witchcraft. Wiccans use magic to benefit the person casting the spell. Wiccans claim they never cast spells that go against the Rule of Three or the Rede. This combination of contacting spirits, along with the socially responsible motto "don't hurt anyone," makes Witchcraft look good, particularly in today's politically correct and religiously tolerant environment. In fact, Witchcraft seems easy to adopt and follow. After all, no one gets hurt. But, as we'll see later, this isn't always the case, and it's not the best reasoning for believing that Wicca is an acceptable religion.

> *The Old Religion is alive and well in modern day Wicca. Using different tools, Wiccans attempt to persuade unnamed spirits (including a Mother/Father God) to work on their behalf, creating a new version of the ancient Sympathetic Magic.*

## ENERGY

Energy, one of the most basic elements of the universe, is also an essential element in Wiccan magic. The first step to understanding the basics of magic from a Wiccan's perspective is to understand their concept of energy. Wiccans believe that there is an energy that flows throughout the universe. This energy is the substance of the creator, the unknowable spirit that is above all spirits. This energy courses through trees, plants, bugs and even people. When witches perform magic, they call on this energy, summoning it for power to control the elements. If they can tap into this energy, they can affect magic in the physical realm. The Wiccan circle provides an area of focus for the energy and the tools manipulate the energy. All magic is performed with one thing in mind—to move the energy that exists in all things to aid the person casting the spell.

> *The Wiccan belief and reliance upon a distant, unnamed energy stands in contrast to the Christian belief that God is personal and involved in our lives.*

To perform any magic, Witches need to bring three things together— the Witch, a Circle, and Magical Tools. These three categories are the essential elements in all magic. To connect to the energy, to direct it rightly and to accomplish their desires, these three areas must be attended to with great detail.

## THE WITCH

Witches believe that in order for the energy to work in the world, it must be coerced and commanded into the natural realm. The witch is the essential element in magic. He or she acts as a conduit for the energy by reaching into its realm, using a variety of tools.

The energy flows from ultimate power that exists in the realm of the unseen, through the witch and the elements, and into our world.

Because the witch plays an important role in Wiccan magic, his or her spiritual life and physical well-being is vitally important. What a witch wears during a ritual or ceremony is also important. Many witches prefer to wear a robe that has been consecrated for rituals. However, some witches believe that clothing prevents their energy from connecting with nature, so they prefer to practice rituals or cast spells completely naked.

## THE CIRCLE

The Wiccan circle is used for celebration and magic. Witches celebrate Sabbats (special holidays), perform magic, and have ceremonies all within a circle.

Witches believe that the circle represents a sacred space between this world and the spiritual realm. In that space they are more connected to the energy and thus they believe they are more able to make magic happen. Circles are usually outside whenever possible. They're often nine to eleven feet in diameter and enclose an altar, which holds the tools. They may be lined with candles that are arranged according to a pentagram. The candles might be at the points of the pentagram, and oriented to the four corners of the earth (North, South, East, and West).

## TOOLS

To create magic, Wiccans use tools that connect with nature. The tools' close connection to nature enables the witch to use them as vessels through which to draw power and energy.[2] Common tools are the pentagram, the wand, a knife (called an athame), a chalice filled with juice or wine, candles, bowls, and incense. Different tools have different uses. The pentagram directs the energy toward the witch. The wand and the knife direct the energy into objects or people.

> *Although some occult stores sell magical tools, most witches don't like buying their tools in a store. Instead, many witches prefer to make their own tools, using natural objects. This serves two purposes. First, the tool made with natural objects continues the connection to the physical world. Second, the time invested in making the tool connects the tool with the witch.*

## THE CEREMONY

Magic takes time, so the entire process is planned. Typically, Wiccans try to cast spells during holidays or phases of the moon—times when there is supposedly more natural energy they can work with.

Because magic involves using power that resides in the spell caster and in nature, the witch has to raise a sufficient amount of power. They do this by dancing, singing or chanting. Another way Wiccans raise the power in a ceremony is to call out names of power. In Wiccan ceremonies, the Old Testament name for God, "Yahweh," is used. Supposedly, if a coven is calling up a spirit they use the name for God to strike fear in the spirit.

> *Wiccan's use the pentagram, and other tools in two distinct ways. In magic, they're used to focus the energy of the Universe (or of the great unnamed creator) to accomplish a specific magic. In Ritual, they're used more in celebration. They show up in rituals honoring New Moons, and Sabbats.*

> *The energy used in Wiccan magic and ritual can be manipulated for good or evil. Since the energy doesn't care how it is used, it can be manipulated either way.*

## Different Kinds of Magic

Wiccans and Satanists categorize their magic into many categories. These aren't just ways to distinguish the purpose behind spells and incantations, they also become the way witches distinguish between each other.

### White

This kind of magic is not intended for harm but helps the witch casting the spell, or another person.

### Gray

Magic that is neither good nor evil is gray. For example, a witch may cast a spell in order to keep someone from casting an evil spell against them.

### Black

Black magic defies the Rede because it is intended for harm. Many Wiccans believe that a true witch doesn't do black magic.

Witches who cast spells only to help are called White Witches. Others who use magic to hurt, or for selfish gain are called Black Witches. Witches who practice both kinds of magic are called Grey Witches.

*People are sometimes confused by the spelling of the word: Magic. Sometimes Wiccans and Satanists spell it Magick instead. The reason for spelling magic with a "k" is to distinguish it from the performance kind of Magic which includes illusion and deception. Wiccans and Satanists are uncomfortable with their magic being associated with this kind of magic which doesn't rely on any power or force, and instead uses human cunning and deception.*

## WITCHCRAFT—SATANIC MAGIC

Wicca claims to use magic only to benefit humanity. Satanism doesn't make that claim. Their use of magic is completely self-focused. Satanic magic can range from simple rituals conducted as if they were worship services to dark ceremonies that include strange sexual practices or summons demons. Satanic magic is often perverted and obscene, dangerous, and extremely harmful. Even Satanists don't encourage people to try their magic, and many of their spell books and writings contain warnings not to attempt them without maturity, practice, and strict preparation.

Like Wicca, Satanists use tools in ritual and magic. In fact, they use many of the same tools the Wiccans use, such as a chalice, candles, etc. Like Wicca, Satanists rely on the power of one's energy to give the magical act potency. The power behind the magic is the emotion and energy of the spell caster. Satanists have three kinds of spells they cast: a spell to get love, a spell that shows compassion on someone, and a spell that is designed to destroy another person.

Unlike Wiccans, Satanists are not limited to performing magic in a formal setting, such as that performed in the midst of a ceremony or ritual. Satanic magic can also be done in a home, in the woods. Anywhere.

The interesting connection between Wiccan magic and satanic magic is in the "calling the corners." In the previous chapter we learned that Wiccans commonly use their pentagrams to call the corners of the earth. In satanic magic and ritual, this same calling process happens. Satanists call upon four principle demons to help them in their magic: Leviathan (representing water), Lucifer (representing air), Belial (representing earth), and Satan (representing fire). Each of these demons is the lord of its element.[3] Calling on these demons (whether they're literally "demons" or are said to represent four evil sides of humanity) is an essential element in satanic witchcraft. In satanic ceremonies, the focal point is the baphomet. They don't worship the baphomet but use it to focus their energy, making their ceremony and magic much more powerful.

Depending on the purpose for the ceremony, Satanists may cast a circle and stand within that (see below for the Circle). Or, they might just meet in a room, using an altar, a baphomet, and their tools. Many of their ceremonies are formatted somewhat like a church service containing readings, prayers, and sacraments.

## THE BLACK MASS

Possibly the most famous satanic ceremony is the Black Mass. Satanists sometimes hold a Black Mass when they seek retribution against another religion. Basically, the Black Mass is another religions worship ritual performed in reverse, intended to be a slap in the face to the offending religion and its adherents. The most popular form of the Black Mass is the Catholic mass performed backward. The satanic church has changed the Catholic Mass into a Black Mass by adding orgies, having sex with dead people, and possibly drinking human blood. While these three are extreme examples, they have been practiced in some Black Masses in the past. [4]

*Anton LaVey was famous for using a naked woman as an altar in all Satanic rituals and magic.*

## THE CIRCLE

In casting spells that require the calling of a demon, the use of a circle is important. In Wicca, the witch generally stands inside the pentagram, and all magic happens within the pentagram. In Satanism, if a pentagram or baphomet is used, the Satanist will either create a circle (which may or may not have a pentagram or baphomet in it) where they stand, or they'll create two circles, one for the person casting the spell and another, specially designed with holy names to contain the demon. This ensures that the person calling on the demon won't get hurt.

> *The calling on and use of demons is an example of Satanism's acceptance of the biblical explanation of the world. Both Satanists and the Bible agree that an unseen world exists and satanic powers can and do influence the physical world.*

## DEMONS

When Wiccans cast spells, they use the elements, the corners of the earth, tools, and energy to persuade and manipulate spirits. Satanists use some of these similar elements, but they call on completely different spirits. Using books like the Necronomicon they call on demons to accomplish magical results. For centuries people have studied and documented thousands of cases of calling on demons. In many cases, people have kept track of the specific names of these demons and their jobs in the spirit realm.

## MAGICAL BOOKS

There are many books available today that promise to lead readers into an otherworldly relationship with spiritual words and magical powers. Many of these books are hoaxes, designed to use the theme of the supernatural in order to get you to buy their stuff. Magic is a very real part of non-christian belief, and accomplishes very real results in the world. The following two books represent two authentic resources available to Witches.

### THE NECRONOMICON

In the early 700s AD, an Arabian poet who had spent years wandering in a desert inhabited by evil spirits composed the Necronomicon. He named the book Al Azif, which is the Arabian name for the sound that insects make and is also believed to be the sound of demons howling at night. He wrote Al Azif just before he was (supposedly) eaten by a huge, invisible monster. Through several translations, this book has taken the name Necronomicon, which can mean the "book of the dead" and the "book of the names of the dead."

A Satanist and writer, named H. P. Lovecraft, claimed to have seen the Necronomicon and brought it to prominence. Some history scholars believe that Lovecraft made up the story of the Necronomicon in order to substantiate his writings. Because no one has ever been able to prove the existence of the Arabian manuscript, some people have created very popular versions of the Necronomicon. These books reflect the "original" Arabian manuscript, or are scary representations of the "original" version. Whatever the history, this book remains an instrumental influence in the development of modern demonology.

The Necronomicon contains spells, rituals, and symbols used for calling on demons for the express purpose of casting spells either for good or evil. Throughout history, books called the Necronomicon have been used with many results. Sometimes people who have used them have gone mad, died mysteriously, or experienced severe demonic oppression. There are many Necronomicons available today written by many different people. Some are accepted as authentic and powerful, others are regarded as literary works, but magically ineffective.

*Unlike the Bible, which claims divine authorship and inerrancy, neither Wicca nor Satanism have a book that is inspired by any deity. Their only "authoritative" sources come from resources that have mysterious histories or are created by the individual.*

BOOK OF SHADOWS

Every witch keeps his or her own book filled with spells, poetry, thoughts, and ideas for ceremonies, called a book of shadows. This book is a lot like a diary. Each witch writes whatever they want in the book to make it a personal record of their rituals and spells. There isn't one single authoritative book of shadows that contains all the correct spells or thoughts. Instead, witches pass down spells and incantations that work to other witches. Sometimes, a coven will create a book of shadows used by the entire coven.

You can't go buy an authentic Book of Shadows, however some publishing houses have published them in an attempt to make Wicca more understandable and acceptable today. Mostly, Witches pass down their favorite and most effective spells to each other, and to members of their covens.

### ANALYZING MAGIC

When we examine the practice of magic in Wicca and Satanism, several connections emerge. Both call on the elements. (Wiccans call on the elements; Satanists call on demons that rule the elements.) Both use similar tools. Both believe in energy that makes magic happen. Both use a pentagram-like symbol in their rituals and magic.

These similarities continue to form a strong bond between Satanism and Witchcraft. In this chapter, the idea of magic reveals several points of Wicca and Satanism that are inconsistent with Christianity and are flatly untrue.

Wicca's and Satanism's reliance on an unseen power that can be manipulated just isn't true. There is no unseen force that is both good and evil. Even if this power did exist, why would it allow itself to be manipulated by humans? It doesn't make sense.

Wiccans and Satanists don't have the exclusive rights of making magical things happen in the physical world. Since the beginning of time, humanity has been trying to manipulate the physical world through spiritual means in order to achieve results that will benefit them. This history is included in Scripture.

In Genesis 41, the power of God in Joseph's dreams stood in contrast with the power of Pharaoh's magicians who attempted to understand Joseph's dreams.

In the book of Exodus, God commanded, through Moses, that Pharaoh free God's people, the Israelites. When Pharaoh refused, God displayed his power and judgment in ten distinct ways through plagues. God's power turned the Nile River into blood, made the sun turn black, and filled the land with frogs. During several of the plagues, the Pharaoh turned to his magicians who were unable to counteract the power of God being poured out on Egypt.

Later, the Old Testament has many references to magicians, and many prophets and teachers urge God's people to stay away from them. These regular references may point to the prevalence of magicians existing in and around ancient Israel.

The one interesting aspect to magic in the Old Testament is the reference to the Urim and Thummim that Moses uses to divine the opinion and will of God (see Exodus 28:30). Scholars don't agree on what these were specifically used for, but their use seems to be for divining the will of God. The priest would pull them out when there was a decision to be made concerning the Israelites and it was directly tied to God. So, even in the smallest of decisions the Israelites would have the knowledge that every decision would be from the mouth of God.

In the New Testament, magic is associated with people who are possessed by evil spirits. Two instances involving the disciples appear in the book of Acts, where the church wrestled with confronting many important issues, including magic. In Acts 8:9-25 and Acts 13:6-12 the disciples deal with sorcerers and practitioners of magic who are working against the disciples. The Bible doesn't mention these people with any surprise, which further makes us assume that magic wasn't uncommon.

God's intervention in human history whether in the Old Testament or in the New, proves his power over magic, divination and any other human attempts to reconstruct or recreate his miraculous work. His miraculous hand is more powerful than magic.

# THE SPIRITS OF WALTER POTTS
## *The Evolution of Humanity*

*W*alter Potts was one of the most notorious people in Clarke City. His practices were well known, and most people were glad that the spell-casting, Christian-hating man had stayed in his home outside the city. Even with his family connection to the founder of the city, Walter never had too many friends.

Five years after Walter Potts went mad, a delivery man passing his house was stopped by an old woman wearing a veil and a black robe. She said that Walter was inside calling out "My father, my father" and setting everything inside of the house on fire. When the deliveryman turned for a second to get his cell phone, the woman had disappeared. Before officials could arrive, Potts' house was completely engulfed in flames. The house burned all night. They never found Walter's body.

All that remained of the house was a blackened fireplace, a few piles of burned furniture, and a large cement slab. No one ever went to Potts' old house. The place still felt dangerous. There couldn't be any good reason to gather there.

"Yeeaahhh, uh-huh. We should not be here. I'm starting to lose my appetite." Jared said, trying to find a level spot for his small cooler.

"I hope you got the right place, Shel. I don't see anyone yet." Paul's confidence in Shelby's information last night was fading. They had driven around for an hour, trying to find a place to hide the car, and a location where they wouldn't be seen. Now, they were not even sure they had the right place.

Jared settled his cooler, opened the lid, and started passing out food. Jared drank chocolate milk, something the rest of the group thought was nasty. Everyone else drank soda.

"Do you think they'll levitate?" Jared asked, gulping his milk. "Maybe they're already meeting but are invisible."

"Maybe they'll sacrifice a cow," Shelby suggested.

"No way! You guys don't think that'll happen, do you?" Mary's shout made the entire group duck for fear of being caught.

Then, slowly, candles lit up the woods. A group of people appeared in a small clearing. None of them talked. They gathered slowly, one at a time. The sun continued to go down. By the time they were all there it was almost dark. As if the real starting time wasn't until the last ray of sunlight had disappeared.

"It's dark enough now. We can get a lot closer," Paul said. Typical. Paul was always wanting to take chances. He moved closer. Everyone followed, including Jared with his chocolate milk.

Covered by hoods, their faces weren't distinguishable. The only light came from the candles they were holding. They encircled one person who was making marks on the ground with white sand. The more sand they dropped, the easier it was to see the pentagram take shape: first the star; then the circle around it. When the circle was finished, the entire group gathered closely around the symbol.

"Do you hear that? Sounds like a hum," Mary said trying to peer around a tree.

"I hear it too," Shelby responded, peering too.

The hum grew louder, and lasted for several minutes. The deep, almost guttural sound pulsated rhythmically from the group. It filled the woods. The teenagers began to feel uneasy.

Someone, who appeared to be the leader, stepped into the center of the pentagram, leading another person into the center too. The leader spoke in an ancient sounding language.

Shelby's voice broke the eerie silence. "Creepy voice. The guy sounds like a funeral director. He sounds familiar. Are you sure they can't see us?"

"Don't you think they'd let us know if they saw us?" Jared took one last gulp of milk, then wiped his mouth with his sleeve.

Paul thought up a plan in case someone saw them. "If they see us, run. Do not look back. Don't say any of our names. Just run. I'll stay in the back and lead them in another direction if they chase us."

The leader raised both hands toward the sky, palms facing in, head turned up. This time he spoke in English. "Great Mother, we have journeyed far though life. Descend upon us we pray. Be in our midst, even as we are in yours. We present ourselves for the sake of our new initiate. Hear us. Fill us. Empower us."

He waved a knife around. First, he touched the knife to the person's head, then to the pelvis, and then the head again. The slow movements amid the chorus of the chanting felt like an eerie worship service.

The chanting grew louder and faster.

"We commit this Spirit to the journey. As all energy is yours, we commit this energy to you." The leader took a bowl from another person in the circle. Holding it in his left hand, he dipped the fingers of his right hand into the water and began touching various parts of the person's body: first the hair; then the mouth, the shoulders, the hands, the knees; and finally, the feet.

This time, the other person standing in the pentagram spoke. "Grant me peace in my journey. Let your energy bring power in my craft. Great Lord and Lady, hold my future secure. As my body is anointed for your glory, so let my rebirth tonight begin my journey on the path you created." As she spoke, candles throughout the group were blown out, one by one, until only the person for whom the ceremony was being performed held a lighted candle.

In the darkness, the entire group spoke. "Make this rebirth spring forth from your glory. Make this rebirth spring forth from your glory. So mote it be."

The leader concluded by saying, "And now you are truly part of our coven, a member of the craft. We welcome you to this new life. So mote it be."

The new person repeated, "So mote it be"

The group responded, "So mote it be."

Holding both hands out to the group the leader said, "Let us celebrate the newest member of our coven. Blessed be."

One by one, the new person went around to each person in the group and relit their candles. With the increasing light, tables could be seen on the outside of the group. Group members walked toward the tables and lit candles there. As the light spread, it revealed that the small group had grown to about seventy-five people. Their hoods were down now and they were grazing at the food tables. This had moved beyond worship and had become a fellowship meal.

"Is that Stephanie's mom?" Mary knew her voice. It sounded familiar.

"Bingo!" Shelby knew the voice too. "This is freaking me out. Can we go now?"

The kids crept backward toward Paul's car. As they walked they could hear the talking of the coven get thinner and more distant. An occasional yell or shout helped them remember that tonight wasn't just an ordinary Wiccan worship service. They added a new member to their group. This was their celebration.

※

LATER THAT NIGHT, Mary laid in bed thinking about the events of the night. Her clock radio was tuned into the local Christian radio

station. She was feeling sick that she had been so close to a witch ritual. She just needed to soak in some praise and worship songs. Besides,
the radio host's voice always put her to sleep.

## DEWITCHING WITCHCRAFT

Both Wicca and Satanism have differing views of the value of humanity, which are tied to their understanding of what a human is. Their
understanding of *what* a human is dictates *how* a human acts while
they're alive.

> Wiccans and Satanists disagree with each other, and even
> within their own religions, about how humans came into exis-
> tence or what their purpose is.

### WICCAN SPIRITISM

While not all Wiccans adhere to the following view of humanity, many
accept these perspectives as true.

BODY

For the Wiccan, the body is a physical shell, the most unimpor-
tant part of the human being. It exists in this world for a variety of
purposes. Wiccans who believe in reincarnation believe that the body
is one of many forms that human spirits can take on. The human
spirit can also come back as animals, insects, spirits, and various other

forms. Though the human spirit can exist on a non-physical plane, the human body cannot.

## MIND

The mind is both physical and non-physical. It is an organ that exists in the physical world, but it contains thoughts and ideas that connect to other planes. If the mind can imagine that other planes of existence exist or can imagine that a Great Spirit exists, then those things must exist. If the mind can imagine it, it must be so.

## SPIRIT

The most important element of the person, the spirit, is a mirror of the Great Spirit (energy) that courses though everything. The spirit is a person's essence. It can travel outside the body and experience other planes of existence. The divine energy that makes up the human spirit makes humanity partly divine. Because they are trapped in their human form, they can't fully realize their divinity. Eventually, though, each human will grasp his divine nature, probably when he dies and becomes part of the Great Spirit.

All humans are a part of the world created by the ultimate energy. They are part of the energy, which makes them part of creation. This connects all humanity together. It also connects humanity to animals and plants, creating a respect and understanding that all of creation is to be revered and respected.

*Wiccans believe that human bodies emanate an energy called an aura. Auras contain a lot of information about someone's health or mood. Wiccan's believe that auras can be read by people either naturally gifted or skilled in reading them.*

## POWER OF HUMANITY

For the Wiccan, human beings are more than just the make-up of three parts. Humans are also on a quest for:

### SELF-UNDERSTANDING

Wiccans are on a quest to know themselves. Through ritual, Wiccans learn who they are and what their destiny is. Tarot cards, divination, magic, and ritual are all keys to self-understanding.

### ULTIMATE EXISTENCE

The cycle of death and rebirth will end when the Wiccan understands enough about the universe to become part of it or to exist on another plane of existence. Being a part of the ultimate existence could just mean walking another plane of existence, or it could mean becoming part of the original life force.

### POWER

Magic and ritual create power for the Wiccan. The more power a witch has, the more effective their magic is. The more magic they perform, the more knowledge they have. Wiccans who believe in using magic both for harm and for good seek to gain more power so their spells will be more effective.

⁂

SELF-UNDERSTANDING AND power are the products of magic and ritual. Magic is used to help witches know themselves better, and rituals help them gain power. This leads to a cycle of magic and ritual, all for the purpose of gaining power over the elements and possibly over other witches.

## SATANIC HUMANISM

Obviously, with the variety of adherent to the Satanic tradition, there are a myriad of beliefs about what a human being is. Basically, Satanists describe humans in the following way.

### HUMANS ARE EVOLVED

Humans have no connection to the divine element. We evolved from tiny microbes into the two-legged, upright creatures we are today.

Because of this, Satanists have a hedonistic view of life. *Because we're evolved and there isn't any tomorrow,* they think, *we should fulfill every desire today.*

## HUMANS ARE ANIMALS

Humans think, act, and behave like intelligent animals. The animal side of humanity is one to be worshiped, explored, and enhanced.

## SURVIVAL OF THE FITTEST

Like evolved animals, humans are all in competition with each other for survival. Each one tries to get what he can while he is alive. We endure an endless series of competitions, attempting to live a long life, not get devoured, and gain wealth and power.

Again, while not all Satanists would adhere to the descriptions above, most would.

This perspective on what a human is dictates how Satanists act while on the earth. Humans should seek their own best. They should do whatever they can to climb higher than other humans. And because whatever comes after this life is an unknown, humans should fulfill every sensual desire possible, using sexual, chemical, emotional, and mental stimulation.

> *"Satan encompasses all of man's inborn qualities, attributes and talents carried to an infinite perfection. The Black Flame of the Dark Prince radiates from a very few contributions born of that immense arena of human imagination. So it follows that only the individual who accepts Satan and who has completed his orientation to Hell carries the potential to recognize and aesthetically appreciate the daemonic donations to an otherwise bland society bulging with restricted, frustrated abilities."*
> – Janet Aquino, wife of the leader of the Temple of Set.[1]

## THE BIBLICAL VIEW OF HUMANITY

In 2 Corinthians 5:1–9 Paul describes humans as being trapped in an earthly tent. Trapped is the perfect word, and accurately describes the tension that humans face. We have eternal elements in us that long to be present with God, but for a short time we are held inside a physical form. Our goal while we're here is to please God with our earthly form. The struggle we face is waiting for the time we inherit the heavenly body that God has prepared for us.

Beyond Paul's excellent description, the Bible gives us some indication of what different parts a human is made of.

### BODY

According to Genesis 1 &2, Adam and Eve's bodies were formed by God's hands. God took dirt and shaped it, and then breathed his breath into them to give them life. We're knit together in our mothers wombs. Our bodies are temples for the Holy Spirit.

This description of the human defines us as people who have an earthly existence, and yet a spark of the divine. We are the image of God meaning that in some way, we look like God. We have the responsibility to glorify Him and honor Him with our earthly tents.

### MIND

In scripture, the mind is often associated with the *soul.* These two parts of the human often defy description by Biblical authors. The mind and soul are the seat of the emotions and will. Oftentimes, the soul is referenced as the entire being. The soul is immortal and in some way lives forever.

### SPIRIT

The human spirit is the core of who we are. The spirit is the life force, and it is the spirit that is often considered the "heart" of the person. This is also a non-material part of the human that lives forever after the death of the earthly tent.

The Biblical description of the human conflicts with Wicca's and Satanism's descriptions. Where Satanism would define the human either as finite (not existing after death) or infinite (existing after death, but in an eternity with Satan), the Bible describes the human as living forever with God in heaven. Wicca tells us that there is a part of the human that lives forever, but in a way we can't understand and with the godhead (either absorbed by it, or existing on a different plane of existence from it). The biblical description tells us that we certainly go and live with God. We exist with Him in heaven.

Clearly the Satanic and Wiccan understanding of humanity conflicts with truth about humanity as revealed in Scripture. Humanity didn't evolve. We're not on a quest for power. We do have a life after this physical one. Our future life in Heaven only depends on our relationship with Christ. We don't have to come back in a series of lives in order to, some day, graduate into an ethereal existence. When we die, we aren't absorbed into an impersonal force. We go and live with God for forever.

Ultimately, Wicca and Satanism don't offer any purpose or hope. They don't offer any answers to people struggling to find their purpose in the world. If you feel awful about your body image, what hope do you have to feel better? If you're struggling with waiting to have sex, what value is there in waiting? The only hope people have in these two beliefs is to either die, and hope that death is a relief or an end to the pain, with no hope of any future.

Our next chapter will take us deeper into the uncertain world of Witchcraft as we learn what they believe happens when we die.

# Chapter 8

# PLANES OF EXISTENCE
## Worlds and Planes

*J*ared sprinted for the old oak doors of the church. He slept through his alarm clock, missed Sunday school, and almost missed church. Thanks to the neighbors' annoying dog barking under his window, he woke up in time to catch the end of the church service. And, hopefully in time to snag lunch with Paul.

He burst through the doors, past the usher who always looked annoyed, around the visitors' table and took the only seat available. The old couple, who always disappeared right after the final "amen," looked at Jared with irritation.

"Cool. Erica's getting baptized today," Jared thought as he surveyed the congregation for the back of Paul's head.

As Jared listened, Pastor Rick added a new element to the baptism. Holding a cup of water in his left hand, he took his right hand, dipped a finger into the water and touched Erica's head.

"Great Lord, grant through this new birth that everything Erica thinks is for your glory."

Rick touched another drop of water to Erica's cheek.

"Grant that everything that comes from her mouth be glorifying to thee. Help her to speak truth and to bring glory to you."

The final drop touched her hands as Pastor Rick spoke, "Be pleased with all her actions. Allow her to be used, and be glorified in everything she does." Then scooping up some water into the palm of his hand and placing it on Erica's head, he said, "Erica Marie Yardley, I baptize you in the name of the Father, the Son, and the Holy Spirit. So let it be. Amen."

AN HOUR LATER, Jared, Paul, and Shelby huddled in the corner table at the usually crowded Green Street Deli.

"Mary's with the Yardleys?" Jared asked, fumbling with his napkin.

"Yup" Shelby responded. "Something about a 'thank you' meal with Mitch and his family."

"Lucky Mary. Cool about Erica today, huh?" Jared asked.

"Yeah, I overheard Mitch talking to her the other day. She's going to start coming to RealWalk more often," Paul added.

"Hey, did anyone notice that Pastor's voice sounded like a funeral director? He's usually so upbeat," Shelby pointed out.

"Forget how he sounded. What about the whole thing with the water? I've been going to that church my whole life. No pastor has ever done anything like that before," Paul responded.

There was a long pause. No one wanted to look at each other. Everyone was wondering the same thing.

SHELBY LAY ON her back in the center of her room with Steph next to her. Lit candles offered the room's only light. The girls lay with their eyes shut arms gently at their sides. Downstairs, Shelby's family sat around the television for the weekly Collins Family movie night. It was a dumb movie anyway. Her little brother had picked it out. So Steph and Shelby had slipped out during the opening scene. Lying there, removed from the only reality she had ever known, Shelby stepped into a new life. Steph led her.

"Now, the first thing you've got to do is relax. Let yourself go. Allow yourself to feel sleepy."

"Allow myself to feel sleepy?" Shelby said, confused.

"Yeah. Relax your body so you feel like taking a nap."

"Steph, it's a little weird to be taking a nap right now."

"Just relax."

"Okay . . . relaxing." Shelby tried as hard as she could to relax. The thought of walking on another plane of consciousness made her nervous, but at the same time intrigued her. Relaxing was difficult . . . like trying to keep from opening presents before Christmas.

"Good, now think of yourself as floating. Imagine that part of you is separated from your body. You're rising up. Now, imagine that you're looking down. You see yourself."

Shelby was confused. "How will I know when this is working?"

"You'll hear a click and you'll be out. It's like a popping sound."

The moment was a conflict of worlds for Shel. She knew she shouldn't get involved in Steph's practices. But this didn't seem so bad. They weren't calling up spirits or casting spells. Steph had been to church with her, it was only right that she got to know what Steph believed. How else could she effectively witness?

"Do you see the cord?" Steph said in a relaxed, sleepy tone.

"The cord? What cord? I'm still trying to relax and imagine the whole floating thing."

"The silver cord. The one connecting you back to your body."

"Steph, this isn't working. I'm not sleepy, and there's something sticking me in the back." Shelby sat up and removed an earring from the back of her shirt. "Hey, I thought I'd lost this forever!" she said, pulling the earring out of her shirt.

Steph sat up too, interrupted from her trip. "OKAY, let's give up. This takes some practice."

"I don't understand what's supposed to happen," Shelby said. "Is this like a magical illusion? You know, like when the lady floats in mid-air and the magician passes a hoop around her?"

"It's nothing like that. This is real. Look, there are many planes of existence," Steph said looking annoyed. "You imagine yourself floating out of your body, and traveling to the astral plane. The astral plane is another form of existence. It exists at the same time as the physical world, but in a totally different way."

"Oh, okay." Shelby's confusion took over. It was all she could think to say.

"It's like this," Stephanie continued. "Right now, we are walking a planet earth made of a material substance. Other worlds exist, but they're made of different substances, different materials. The Bible even talks about it. I think Mitch called it the spirit world. Same thing, different name."

Shelby was intrigued. She hadn't thought about it that way before. "You've been there?"

"Yep. There are things on the astral plane you could never imagine. Images that blow your mind."

"Is there another way to get there? All of this relaxing and floating stuff just doesn't seem to work for me."

"You just need to practice, Shel. You've got to try over and over before you can get out of your body."

The girls lay back down again for another try. Shelby wasn't into it, and kept distracting Steph. Soon, the two were lying on their sides on Shelby's twin beds and giggling over the guys at Clarke City High. Jared and Paul kept coming up in the conversation.

"Ew! You think he's cute?" Shelby shouted.

"Don't you?" Steph said, looking in her bag for nail polish.

"I've known Jared long enough now. He feels more like my brother. I wouldn't go out with him or anything."

"I would. Why not?"

"Well, I guess love is a crazy thing. You never know who you're gonna hook up with. But Jared? Ick." Shelby continued, telling Steph a series of stories about Jared and some of his more memorable, stupid moments. The girls talked late into the night until both were exhausted from laughing and telling stories about their lives. Eventually, Shelby passed out.

Steph lay in the other twin bed staring at sleeping Shelby. As she lay there, she quietly sang a rhyme in an ancient language, like a mother soothing a sleeping baby. Soon, Steph was asleep.

## DEWITCHING WITCHCRAFT

### WORLDS AND PLANES

What would it be like to travel to different places anytime you wanted? You wouldn't need to pack a suitcase or bring food. You wouldn't need airplane tickets. Ahead of you lay places you could only dream of, places like heaven, although not actually heaven. Places where other beings dwelled. All you needed to travel to these different worlds was a comfortable place to lie and maybe a few ritualistic tools to help your travel or enhance your consciousness. With enough time to drift into a semi-dream state, you would slide easily out of your body and onto the astral plane.

When you discard the biblical belief of heaven and hell as the only possible planes of existence (other than the physical world), the result is a wide variety of beliefs and ideas. The result in Wiccan and Satanist belief systems is that spirits can exist on several different levels, and the physical world is only one plane of existence. Wicca and Satanism believe differently about these places, and even differently about how a being exists after the physical world.

## WICCAN PLANES OF EXISTENCE

In Wicca, people can "exist" in a variety of ways and in a myriad of locations. Obviously, physical form is our primary understanding of existence. Humans live in the realm of the sensory experience. We see, feel, touch, and taste—all with our physical senses. However, this is only one plane of existence, the only one we know or completely understand.

Wicca doesn't have a defined understanding of what actually exists beyond our sense experience—so Wiccans rely on theory, ideas, and mystery to describe other planes of existence. They also rely on ancient writings and current thought to create their views of both the afterlife and other planes of existence. But, there isn't much agreement about what other planes of existence there really are. Depending on the Wiccan or the coven, different groups believe different things.

*It's important to remember Wicca's understanding of the idea of energy that we previously discussed. Travel throughout some of these planes is easier because both the witch and the planes are made from the same energy, which flows from the ultimate creator.*

### SEVEN PLANES OF EXISTENCE

Wiccan author Raven Grimassi offers a comprehensive list concerning planes of existence. His list gives a complete view of the possible places where Wiccans believe spirits can live. Some might agree with this list, others might agree that an astral plane exists along with one or two others. Still others might reject this list entirely and fall back on the idea that, beyond our physical understanding of the universe, everything else is mostly unknowable.

Wiccans believe that energy vibrates at many different frequencies and speeds. Energy that vibrates at lower frequencies and speeds remains more solid, and creates physical things like physical bodies and planets and things on the planets. Energy that vibrates at higher speeds and frequencies creates other things, other kinds of matter and other worlds. Each of these seven planes of existence describes a different way energy vibrates to create an "existence."

Here's a brief explanation of each of these planes:

### THE ULTIMATE PLANE

This is the plane where the ultimate deity exists. This realm is unknowable—human minds can't comprehend it. This realm is beyond God, the gods, or any concept we could have about God. It's the plane from which every created thing came.

### THE DIVINE PLANE

This plane could also be called the divine plane of consciousness. It's believed that this is where the god and goddess live. It's also where some of the lesser gods exist.

### THE SPIRITUAL PLANE

This is the land where "beings of light" exist and are no longer bound to the cycle of reincarnation. These spirit beings could be considered angels, but could also be called ascended masters, spirit guides, etc.

### THE MENTAL PLANE

The thoughts and actions flow from the divine plane and into the mental plane. Eventually, these thoughts flow from the mental plane and into the realm of our physical existence.

### THE ASTRAL PLANE

This is the plane of possibility. Ideas and images either from a plane above or from the physical world begin to form into a "real" substance here. This plane shouldn't be thought of as "real" in the way we understand realness. Instead, the astral realm is made up of an indescribable, somewhat physical and yet somewhat spiritual substance.

## THE ELEMENTAL PLANE

This plane takes the energy from the astral plane and brings the image from the astral plane into the material world. This is more a plane of transition. Things thought of in other planes and materializing in the astral plane are brought to existence through this plane.

## THE MATERIAL PLANE

This is the physical world that you and I know and experience every day. It's considered the lowest plane of existence not because we're considered low creations, but because it's the lowest level of vibration. Energy is believed to move at its slowest on this plane. [1]

*An equally popular understanding of the "planes of existence" believed by many Wiccans is the concept of the "Three Tiered Universe." The overworld (sky, heavens), middleworld (Earth), and underworld (a land under the surface of the earth) are believed to be the basic construction of the world. When you read Scripture (especially the Old Testament), this view seems to be the most accepted perspective on the way the universe is constructed. This view was also held by ancient Mesopotamian religions, and was popular in Ancient Greece.*

Some of these planes are easily "tapped into." Wiccans call on spirits (existing on the spiritual plane) or invoke the gods (from the divine plane) and even travel on the astral plane. The key idea here is Wicca's understanding of the *accessibility* of these realms of existence. Their world isn't partitioned into segments closed in by huge brick walls. The divisions among these worlds are murky, and easily crossed. By traveling to these planes, Wiccans believe they gain wisdom and understanding. The more travel, the wiser the witch.

There is more than one way to travel to these planes. Divination *is the process of contacting one of these planes through the use of* stones or tarot cards. *In this case, Wiccans don't actually travel outside their bodies; instead, they use tools and instruments to get the spiritual world to come to their world. Sometimes this includes actually requesting the presence of a spirit. Other times, it just means opening a "door" to the other plane of existence to gain wisdom or knowledge not known to the witch.*

## SPIRITUAL TRAVEL

It's nearly impossible for any person from any religion to completely explain what our non-physical bodies are like. The best word to describe the substance of spirit bodies according to Wiccans is *ethereal.* An ethereal substance is partially physical, but not completely physical. It's partially spiritual, but not completely spiritual. In order to travel to another plane, the believer has to take on this ethereal form. Supposedly, this is done through entering a dreamlike state and imagining yourself floating out of your body. Wiccans believe that some people are born to travel in ethereal bodies, and the process of moving into this state is easy for them.

Traveling to any of these planes requires either a natural ability or an acquired skill. It requires that the witch get in sync with the energy that vibrates through everything. Wiccans believe the energy that is in the different worlds is also in the human body. They also believe that they have another, ethereal, body that they can't see, and that this energy flows through that body as well.

This other body is most accessible to people when they're in between being awake and asleep. In this semi-dream state the other form is released from the physical form and free to look around. There isn't any adequate explanation of what this astral body is like or a good explanation of what happens to people when they're wandering around in their astral bodies.

When wandering the astral plane, Wiccans say that a living person differs from a dead person in this plane because living people are connected to their physical bodies through a silver cord. Beings on the astral plane are able to move freely to other locations around the planet. They're able to move at the speed of thought.

*The one time each year when it is believed that the door between the physical world and the world of the dead is open is on October 31. Wiccans call this Samhain, which dates back to an ancient Celtic tradition. They hold special celebrations honoring the dead, and attempt to contact dead relatives.*

*Wiccans who believe the astral plane theory say that ghosts are humans walking the physical world in their astral body. Since these bodies are of another substance, they appear shadowy, unclear or in forms that we can't comprehend.*

## SATANIC OTHER WORLDS

Many Satanists would loudly proclaim, as LaVey did, that humans do not have a soul or an afterlife. In fact, they'd more likely say that the way a human lives after death is through their offspring. People live forever in the memories of their children.

Beyond the atheistic beliefs that are the hallmark of many satanic groups, trying to decipher the varying Satanist beliefs about different planes is nearly impossible. Satanists who don't believe the LaVey theories tend to believe that there is a realm beyond the physical world where spirits (including demons, unnamed spirits and possibly angels) exist, and where the spiritual substance of the human goes when they die. Views as to how many of these places exist, what they are like, what you do when you get there differ depending on the Satanist.

Satanists who believe in other spiritual realms believe that the Christian church created a negative view of hell to scare people who didn't believe in the church's teachings. They also believe that hell is a good place—a place that fills all the senses—and that those who inhabit it enjoy being there. In fact, many Satanists believe that heaven and hell might really be one place where all spirits go when they die. It's also the place where demons and other spirits live.

For Satanists, traveling back and forth from the physical world to the spiritual realm isn't as easy as it is for Wiccans. Satanists believe that it's not possible to travel to this place and come back. However, they do believe that it is possible to call on demons from this plane to seek advice and assistance, as in magical rituals. (See chapter 6 for more on this.) The process of tapping into this realm involves dangerous Black Magic, and a variety of spells, to call upon demons living in this unseen, middle world.

> *Satanists committed to Black Rituals (similar to Black Magic) have spell books designed to unlock the doors between the physical world and the demonic world. Aleister Crowley supposedly found such a book. Today, there are dozens of these books that claim not only to contain magical spells, but also to create portals that give demons passage into our world.*

## WHAT CHRISTIANS BELIEVE

Spirit bodies and the afterlife are two issues that Christians have wrestled with since the beginning of the church. Even the disciples couldn't grasp the kind of body Jesus had when he rose from the dead. Are heaven, hell, and earth woven together? Can people pass back and forth between these worlds? And what of the bodies that we have when we die? Are they completely transparent? Or are they both spirit and material?

We can't say that we know *exactly* what heaven will be like. We can't say that we know *exactly* what our heavenly bodies will be like. However, using Scripture we can piece together a few facts.

## SPIRIT BODIES

Throughout the Bible, we find people who wondered what the substance of their bodies would be like on the other side of their physical understanding of the world. Probably the most popular and important explanation of our spiritual bodies is in 1 Corinthians 15, where Paul related our spiritual bodies to Jesus' resurrected body. Paul didn't explain what our bodies would look like. Instead, he said that they would be like Jesus' resurrected body— one of physical substance and yet able to move quickly to different locations.

## HEAVEN AND HELL

The Bible describes heaven as a place that really exists. It's referred to as the place where God dwells (Isa. 57:15, 66:1) and the place where the spirit of a believer goes when the human body dies (Phil. 3:20-21). There are loads of passages in the Bible that tell us that heaven is the place where Christians go when they die.

Hell is described throughout the Bible as an existence that is uncomfortable. It's called a fiery furnace (Matt. 13:49) and a place of torment (1 Thess. 1:9). The Bible tells us that it is a place where the soul is destroyed (Matt. 10:28). And where Satan will ultimately be sent (Rev. 20:10) and demons will be bound (Jude 6).

Different worlds and planes. Various locations where spirits can exist. It doesn't involve just energies and invisible spirits, but also the human. What happens when someone dies? Do they go and live in another world? How do they exist after death? In the next chapter, we'll learn how the concept of the various worlds and planes are directly tied to the afterlife.

# THE CEREMONY
*The Afterlife*

*T*he glow of the fire ring lit up the clearing. Hooded figures gathered around the perimeter, chanting. Inside the ring was a circle with symbols and pictures. There was one of Mary, Paul, Jared, and Shelby. Under each picture lay an object: Mary's lost ring, one of Paul's shoelaces, an empty carton of Jared's milk, and a couple strands of Shelby's hair.

Stephanie began. "Let us connect tonight with these spirits. Powers of Earth, Air, Fire, and Water, fill us! Renew us! We join with the great power. Grant us power over these followers of the way."

Slowly, Steph made pentagrams in the air over each picture. With each pentagram she repeated, "Guide them into *our* way. Lead them into *our* path. Bring them into *our* fold."

As her disciples watched, Steph took each object and picture rolling each one into a tube. As Steph tied each tube with a short piece of twine, she instructed her coven like a young pastor teaching her congregation about spiritual warfare.

"These Christians stand in our way. We're not fighting these people physically. We're fighting them with our power. If we get just one of them, our power grows stronger. We claim all of them tonight. Let us direct our energy and power toward bringing them into our coven."

Motioning to the group, Steph's words encouraged them in their next step in the ceremony. "Enter the circle, and renew your commitment to our cause, and to ridding our city of these believers. We will have them."

One at a time, the hooded believers entered the ring, cut their fingers with the knife and dripped their blood on each of the rolled up pictures. Their words filled the woods:

"Grant us power.

Grant us strength.

Grant us wisdom."

As the last person exited the ring, Stephanie stood in the center. Slowly she tossed each picture into the fire.

"We have sealed this. The bond cannot be broken. Let this power live. Let us be used to finish this work. We will not rest. With this power we will conquer. When you are discouraged, remember the power tonight. Remember the fire. Remember your blood, used to seal the bond between the seen and unseen. We will reign. They will join us."

One at a time, they disappeared into the night. They moved back to their cars, quickly hiding their cloaks in the trunk.

Steph bowed alone in the center of the fire ring caught up in a moment of worship. Her hooded cloak fell over her so she looked like a black mound in the center of fire. She listened to the sound of the fire roaring as the night wind whistled through the trees. The moment dripped with evil. Steph felt power surge through her blood. Eyes gently closed. Bowing east. She slowly breathed the words, "All hail. . . . All hail. . . . All hail. . . ."

❧

THE GREEN STREET Deli was one of the few good places to eat in Clarke City. Pastor Rick, Mitch, and Police Chief Collins met there regularly for lunch. Chief Collins attended Clarke City Community Church and met with Pastor Rick each week for prayer and a short Bible study. Afterward, they would invite Mitch to lunch. Mitch looked forward to these lunches. He felt validated as a valuable member of the church staff to be aligned with these two influential members of the community. At times like this, Mitch felt in the loop. Over turkey and bacon hoagies, Chief Collins would often let the guys in on any unusual police pursuits or domestic fights.

"We're finding them all over now. It's the same each time. The thing is split wide open. Blood everywhere. A pentagram carved in the head that matches the pentagram the animal is laying on. And they always take the tail."

"Do you have any idea who's doing this?" Pastor Rick asked.

"We don't," Chief Collins replied, picking a piece of turkey from between his teeth, "but we know there's a lot of 'em. At each scene, we've found the area around the animal all stomped down. It's as if they throw a party after killing it."

"This is pure Satanism," Mitch jumped in, eager to impress, "the pentagram carved in the head, the missing tail, the pentagram on the ground, these are all a part of a satanic ritual. I know what I'm talking about. We've been covering this issue during RealWalk."

"Yeah, Shelby mentioned something about that. I was hoping you guys could give me a little insight into what we're dealing with."

Mitch saw this as the perfect opportunity to become a key member of the investigation and possibly the community. He told Chief Collins all he knew about Satanism and Wicca. Pastor Rick was silent, except for an occasional nod.

"What do you suppose they're doing with the tails?" Collins asked.

"I'm not sure. Maybe it's a trophy?"

Pastor Rick finally jumped into the discussion. "Actually, a group like this would keep the tail as a symbol of power. If they possess something from the animal, then the animal's power becomes their own."

"Power?" Collins said. This was news to him.

"Well, yes. That's the idea. They'll use any living thing in a ritual, especially if they're casting a spell. A life force used in spell casting makes the spell stronger. They like to use an object belonging to the person they're casting the spell on. If they don't have something belonging to that person, any living thing will do."

Collins interest was piqued. "That explains it."

"Explains what?" Rick asked.

"Mitch, we found a picture of you wrapped around a tail at one of these sites. We weren't sure what they were doing with it, but apparently you've ticked somebody off."

"I've been talking a lot about satanic cults at our youth meetings. Maybe someone didn't like what I said."

"Could be. Be careful, Mitch. So far they are only killing animals, but they're believed to be cold, calculating, and dangerous. If they've turned their attention on you, who knows. . . ." Unsure of the right thing to say, Collins' words fell off. Turning to Pastor Rick, he continued, "Hey Rick, why don't you come down to the station next Tuesday morning and fill our guys in on some of this stuff. It might help the investigation."

"You bet. Call my secretary and have her put it on my calendar. Gentlemen, I've got to get going," Rick said, standing up quickly and heading for the door.

⁂

RICK GAVE MITCH a ride back to the church. After a few minutes of silence, he abruptly turned and said, "Mitch, you like Collins, don't you?"

"Well, yeah," Mitch responded. "He's been extremely supportive of the youth group."

"Then why would you try and prevent him from being objective about these cow killings. The man has a job to do, and all of that talk about Satan being behind the killings only makes it harder for him to see what's really happening."

"What's really happening," Mitch began, almost with a tone of sarcasm, "is that people are involved in satanic ritual killings. I think it's pretty clear. I think Collins already suspected that."

Rick pulled his Cadillac into his parking space and turned off the engine. He moved his heavy body sideways so he could face Mitch. "No, what's clear is that cows are dying. Yes, it's scary. Yes, Collins has a job to do. But to say that Satan is behind it? Well, that's just stupid. And to say that out loud at the deli? That was stupid too."

"I'm not sure I'm getting you here, Rick."

"Did you know that one table over from us there was a couple who I know are witches? Well, you'd probably call them witches. That's not what I'd call them. Anyway, I'm sure they heard you talking about your 'Satan killed the cows' idea. Don't you suppose that your comments hurt their feelings?" Rick put the car in park, got out, and headed for the church.

"I guess," Mitch said, jumping out of the car and following behind. "But this is truth we're talking about. I think we can stand for something, even if it offends people."

"I guess that depends on how you define truth," Rick shot back. "Mitch, not everyone sees it like you do. Some people believe that blaming cow deaths on good-natured citizens is bigotry. You're not a bigot, are you Mitch?"

Mitch didn't respond.

"No, you're a good man. Tolerance, Mitch. You need to learn tolerance. Let Collins do his job. Don't pack his head with silly ideas of satanic killings. You don't know what's going on. You should keep your mouth shut—unless, you *want* to be called a bigot. If so, you're on the right track."

Mitch didn't have time to respond, nor did he know what to say. A quick stop to pick up his phone messages, and Rick disappeared into his office. Mitch drug his wounded spirit into his office. RealWalk was tonight, and there was a lot left to plan.

※

"A FEW THINGS you need to know about Satanism before we close tonight. As the worship band comes up to lead our closing song, I want you to hear a couple of things. First, remember that Satan doesn't . . ."

Mitch's words seemed to go on and on. Jared had heard this before. His mind wandered. As he glanced around the room, Shelby's necklace caught his attention. He whispered to get her attention

"Psst! Shel? Cool necklace. Can I see it?"

Without talking, still focused on Mitch, Shelby took off her necklace and handed it to Jared, who began admiring, then studying it.

"Shelby, do you know what this is? This is a pentagram!" It was difficult to keep his voice at a whisper.

"Shhh!" she whispered putting her finger to her mouth. "It's not what you think. And it's not evil. Give it back and stop freaking out," Shelby demanded.

"Shel, you know you shouldn't be wearing it! Why are you doing this?" Jared whispered, back in control.

"I'm wearing it because it's cute. It doesn't mean anything to me, Jared. It's just a beautiful piece of art. Look at the cool way they stained the wood. See the bumps on the edges? They're carved into the wood. Don't they look like real beads?"

"Take it off, Shel. This isn't funny!" Jared was getting scared.

Shelby acted like she couldn't hear Jared. She closed her eyes and raised her hands as the worship team played the final song. When

RealWalk ended, Shelby headed for the parking lot where her mom waited to take her home.

## DEWITCHING WITCHCRAFT

When you die, what happens?

No one knows exactly what happens when you die. People can tell you their *theories*. They can interpret biblical passages and other philosophies and give you an informed opinion about what they think will happen—but no one knows for sure. *Because* no one knows with an exact certainty, we rely on ideas and concepts that we form about the unseen world, our "spirit bodies," and the universe. We rely on what we already believe about the existence of a god—either the all-powerful God of the Bible, an unnamed force, or another all-powerful being—as the source for our knowledge of the afterlife.

What you believe about the nature of humanity, and what you believe about the different planes of existence beyond the physical impact your view of the afterlife. If you don't believe that there is any other existence after the physical world, then obviously there is no afterlife. If you believe that the human is made primarily of spirit, or that there really are other forms of existence, then clearly the afterlife exists, and your spirit body exists within that context. Both Wicca and Satanism have different ideas about the afterlife, and they're based primarily on their understandings about the various planes of existence, and how humans exist in those different planes.

## Two Important Elements Affecting the Afterlife

While Wicca and Satanism differ on the way beings exist after death, both agree, at some level, on the idea of energy, and how negative or positive energy affects them in the afterlife.

### Karma

The energy that flows from the god (or source of all creation) flows into all things—living and inanimate, making every *thing* ultimately spiritual. This energy doesn't just flow into things, but also flows *through* all things and into other planes of existence. The entire universe is fueled by this energy. The entire universe is made of this energy. This energy *is* the universe.

This energy is subject to the forces of cause and effect. An action on any object causes an effect throughout the universe. Karma looks a lot like the Rule of Three. If you do good things, you create good energy and you end up having a good life. If you live badly, then you create negative energy and you end up either paying the price for that bad energy or you have to pay back the bad energy with good energy by paying restitution or changing how you live. Paying back the negative energy is called paying the *karmic debt*, which may mean that you are placed in the path of someone else's negative energy.

Karma and the Rule of Three are almost exactly alike. Except for one difference. The Rule of Three is limited to specific actions. For the Wiccan, casting a spell to harm someone will result in harm coming back on the spell caster. Being mean to someone will result in someone being mean back (three times as bad). The Rule of Three is a principle of specific return, based on an action.

The Rule of Three is dependent on an action, but karma is a life force that is part of the force of the universe. A series of good choices—including how you treat other spirits, how you act, your attitude, and a host of other actions—affect your karma. Good choices affect your energy, making your energy a positive force in the universe. Karma is part of the cause-effect that Wiccans believe orders the entire universe. Karma exists no matter what you do (unlike the Rule of Three, which is in effect based on human actions). Your karma follows you through life.

Your karma determines your afterlife, and it's closely tied to the concept of reincarnation. If you've created good karma throughout your life by living a good life (by doing good things or contributing to the good of humanity, etc), then it's possible that you will progress to another level of existence. If, however, you have created bad karma, it can lead in another direction. All of this is linked to the idea of reincarnation.

*It's difficult to decipher exactly what Satanists believe about karma. Many discard it as a silly Wiccan idea of how the universe operates. However, some Satanists believe that there is a force that one creates, and the force has an impact on your life or afterlife. Satanists differ from Wiccans by holding to an entirely different standard of good and evil that humans create. In other words, a Satanist may define a "good life" or an "evil life" by an entirely different value system than the Wiccan would.*

REINCARNATION

Reincarnation is a continual rebirth of the soul into many different physical forms over an indefinite period of time. Some of the forms a soul is reborn into can be human, but they don't have to be. Souls can be reborn into insects, trees, animals, or anything else that has life. The soul goes through these successive births and rebirths in order to learn lessons. With each life, the soul gets progressively wiser, and prepares for a higher plane of existence. After several lives, the soul knows everything it's intended to know, and then goes on to live with the gods.

So the Wiccan believes they attain the "afterlife" after going through a spiritual process of refinement. They might reincarnate if their soul needs to learn new lessons, or if the universe needs them in another life for a specific purpose. They might reincarnate as a "lower form of existence" if they have a karmic debt, or if they've been especially bad in their previous life.

The idea of karma and reincarnation create a picture of the afterlife that is shrouded with a great unknown. No Wiccan knows whether they'll come back, what they'll come back as, or when they'll graduate to another plane of existence. This unknown creates a constant uncertainty about the afterlife.

> *The belief in karma and reincarnation leads to a lifestyle of salvation based on works. The better a person acts the better their chances are of coming back in a higher state of existence after death. This contrasts with the loving God of the Bible, who offers salvation and an afterlife based on relationship.*

## THE WICCAN AFTERLIFE

In the previous chapter we learned about the seven planes of existence that some Wiccans believe exists. Other Wiccans believe in the overworld, middleworld, underworld structure of the universe. They may believe that after death, the spirit goes on to another plane of existence (most often the astral plane) or to the overworld, where the spirit exists either with the creator spirit or in a shadowy existence with other spirits. Obviously, this all depends on one's karma and whether the soul of the person is destined to come back for another incarnation in a physical form.

If a soul isn't destined for rebirth, where does it go? What happens when the human form dies, and the invisible part of the human lives on? Wiccans fall into two categories in their belief in the afterlife. Either the soul goes and lives on the astral plane and waits for the next level of existence, or the soul goes to Summerland, a place of eternal summer.

## THE LADDER OF THE AFTERLIFE

The Wiccan ladder is an easy way to understand the varying degrees of the afterlife. The three most popular Wiccan beliefs of the afterlife are the ascending ladder, the ascending-descending ladder, and the one-step ladder.

## THE ASCENDING LADDER

If a Wiccan's karma is good and they aren't slated to return to the physical world, there are a host of possibilities as to where they will go next—and all of them are related to the seven planes of existence. The soul can ascend up a series of existences based on its karma. Obviously, the soul wouldn't exist on the elemental plane or the mental plane. However, it is possible for the soul to exist on the astral plane and even the divine plane or the spiritual plane.

It's not clear how the soul progresses through these planes, and it's not clear what exactly the soul does in the afterlife.

## THE ASCENDING-DESCENDING LADDER

The ascending-descending ladder theory of the afterlife looks remarkably like the Christian understanding of heaven and hell. The Three Tiered Universe (overworld/middleworld/underworld) theory dates back to the Old Religion, and early humanity's way of explaining how the universe operates. The ancient understanding of evil was typically related to the concept of a land under the earth where evil dwelt. And, the idea of a place where the gods lived was usually assigned to the sky or heavens.

This ancient understanding of the world exists today. Based on one's karma, the soul goes on to live in the afterlife in one of two places: in the heaven or in a place "above" where the divine force lives, or in a place of punishment where evil resides.

This imitation of the Christian understanding of the afterlife isn't by accident; rather, it's a theory that makes sense.

*Wiccans who believe in a shadowy existence after death are actually holding to an Old Testament understanding of the afterlife. During Old Testament times, most people believed that after death the soul went to live in a shadowy place called* sheol. *In the New Testament, the Sadducees who believed in the afterlife (not all of them did) believed in the concept of sheol.*

## THE ONE-STEP LADDER

The one-step ladder relies on karma as the determining factor for whether or not a soul is reincarnated or goes on to live in Summerland. Summerland is glorious, full of joy, harmony, peace and tranquility. According to the one-step ladder theory, it is the only place the soul can go in the afterlife. Spirits in Summerland enjoy peace with each other, they enjoy feasts, and they have a non-stop party.

If you're familiar with Greek mythology, you'll recall the Greek belief that when someone dies, they go to a place called Elysium. The Greek concept of Elysium is much like the Wiccan understanding of Summerland. In fact, many Wiccan scholars use the Greek concept of Elysium to explain their belief in Summerland. It's entirely possible that the Wiccan belief in Summerland is borrowing Greek mythology of the afterlife.

*Wicca's animistic beliefs mean that even rocks and trees have spirits living in them that live forever. Makes you wonder . . . do rocks live forever?*

## THE SATANIC AFTERLIFE

Like Wiccans, Satanists believe a variety of things about the afterlife. And, like Wiccans, Satanists' beliefs about the afterlife are based on their understandings of the different worlds that exist beyond the physical world.

## No Afterlife

Those who think that Satan is just an idea, and the name Satan actually represents the darker side of humans rather than a literal being, believe that death is the end of your existence. There is no belief that the soul or anything else lives beyond the physical form.

## An Eternal Something

Those who believe that Satan is a literal being and exists in a place called hell, believe that you go to hell when you die. They believe that the Christian understanding of hell as a bad place is a construction of lies made up by the church. They believe that hell is actually a good place. And some Satanists believe that everyone goes to hell when they die.

Spirits who live in hell enjoy uninterrupted access to Satan and live with an unending fulfillment of sensual desires. Satanists equate hell with the Wiccan idea of Summerland, but a hundred times more sensual and sense filled.

## Heaven, Hell and The Afterlife

Obviously, everything in the Bible regarding the afterlife stands in direct contrast to the teachings of Wicca and Satanism. Wicca's understanding of the afterlife as a ladder we climb depending on our karma or on a successive number of incarnations opposes the Bible's explanation of the afterlife. Satanism's acceptance of the idea of a hell, yet a total revision of the idea of hell, mocks the biblical description of the afterlife existence without God.

It's important to remember what I said at the beginning of this chapter. No one knows with exact certainty what happens when we die. While the Bible paints general pictures of the afterlife, there aren't any specifics. We know that Jesus promised us a mansion; we know that the streets are supposedly paved with gold. But the texture of heaven and hell, the exact specifications and dimensions, the smells and the surroundings aren't specified in the Bible.

Earlier, we learned that one of the predominant beliefs about the afterlife in Old Testament was that at death all souls traveled to a shadowy place called sheol. However, Old Testament Scripture indicates that the world was divided into three distinctive sections— heaven, hell, and earth—much like ancient Pagan understandings of the universe. There were different levels of both heaven and hell reserved for those who were especially good or especially bad.

Isaiah's words in 66:1 explain that the dwelling place of God is thought to be heaven, a place above in the sky (Ps. 123:1). Scripture speaks of God looking down (Ps. 102:19). In the New Testament, the idea of heaven and hell is an interesting understanding. Hebrews 8:1 speaks of Jesus being the High Priest in heaven, who is at the right hand of God. Above all of this, the Bible specifically states that God is the creator of these places (Heb. 1:10).

Of heaven, Paul writes that the sufferings that believers endure on earth will be surpassed by the reward they'll receive in heaven (Rom. 8:18?19). Paul also writes that the bodies we have now won't compare to the bodies we'll inherit when we stand with God in heaven (Phil. 3:20?21). In that same passage Paul points out that the believer's citizenship is in heaven, and an earthly citizenship doesn't compare to the one that awaits.

Hell is often talked about in the New Testament as a place where demons reside, or as the place that seems to be the exact opposite of heaven. Of the numerous passages that describe hell, Matthew 13:38–42 and Luke 16: 19–31 offer a complete understanding. Hell is a place of torment and pain, a place of separation from the goodness of God. Ultimately, everything in hell is tossed into the Lake of Fire, where the torment increases and the separation from God is agonizing.

Of course, we're talking about generalities here. Even as Jesus described heaven and hell using stories and parables, he did not give us a complete description. Heaven is possibly the most indescribably beautiful place, and the torment of hell is impossible to capture in words. We're left only with those broad strokes, and the promise that a glorious home awaits, along with a new body and the unending presence of God, for those who follow him.

## BIBLICAL KARMA, REINCARNATION, AND GOD'S DECISION

It doesn't take a biblical scholar to understand that God's will for believers is to make their own decision to follow him. You don't need to know deep biblical theology to know that in the biblical explanation of the world, ideas like karma and reincarnation aren't consistent with God's plan for humans.

Ultimately, humans are left with a fairly simple decision. It's too simple to be accepted by Wiccans, because they're interested in denying the monotheistic truth about God, and the power of the transformation that Jesus makes in our lives. It's too simple to be accepted by Satanists, because they're intent on denying God has any power and interested in creating a religion that opposes Christianity.

Believers are left with the simple choice to adhere to the biblical description of what a human is, what worlds and planes exist that we can't see, and where the soul goes when it leaves the body. It's a simple decision based on faith and trust that God does not lie in his Word, and that he tells us the truth, even today.

# THE FIRE RING
*Holidays*

ou know Mary, I've been to RealWalk, and I've even been on a retreat with your church. Would you be willing to come with me to a church thing?" Steph asked looking over at Mary.

"I get together with some other kids from our school. We worship kind of like my mom does, but it's a little different. For us, worship is a very personal thing."

Mary suddenly realized that they were just outside Clarke City. "Where are we?" She was beginning to get scared.

"Sorry I'm driving so fast. We're kind of late."

"Tonight? We're going tonight? I've got homework. I'll be in a lot of trouble if my parents find out. I can't go tonight." Mary was in a panic.

"Too late. We're here," Steph said grinning at Mary.

Steph slammed on the brakes, and her car almost slid into another car as it came to rest near the thick woods.

Climbing out, Steph walked over to Mary's side. Opening the door, she grabbed Mary tightly by the arm and said, "Come on. I want you to see this."

"What choice do I have?" Mary said, climbing slowly out of the car.

Just through the woods, Mary could see a flashlight casting a dim light on the trees.

It offered just enough light for Mary to make out what was happening. Two kids she'd never seen before were there. One was carving at the body of a calf. His hands and arms were dripping with blood. Another guy, holding the tail in his hands, looked directly at Mary.

She could feel Steph standing close behind her. In one instant, everything became clear.

"Mary, whatever you think it is we do, it's more than you can imagine. We're doing things that will make a difference. We're trying to change the world. We want you to be a part of us. We know the story of your life. We know your future. Your future is with us."

Mary turned to face Steph. She looked like the girl Mary had gotten to know and like, but there was something different about her now. A cloud of darkness enveloped Steph. Hatred seethed from her being. Mary began to feel heavy. She sensed her moving closer. Hands rested on her shoulders.

"You Christians are completely out of touch. You proclaim freedom, but your God makes you his slave. You really think you can change the world? Name one thing your youth group has done to make this world a better place. Mary! You can be a part of something wonderful. You really can change the world. We need you. Most of all, you need us." Stephanie's words slid out.

Noticing Mary was looking for an escape, Stephanie continued her onslaught. "Do you really want to live the rest of your life like a mindless idiot? Can't you think for yourself? Do you have to ask permission to do everything, including deciding what you believe?" Stephanie's voice got louder, more pressing. "Serve with us, Mary. Walk with us. We serve a king who makes us kings. We will rule with him."

More kids arrived, moving silently to the sanctuary without walls. Mary could make out faces now: Jennie, the quiet girl in her English class; Kyle, her geometry study date from last week; and even Pete, Pastor Rick's oldest son.

"See? You know us, Mary. You're around us all the time. We have more power than you could imagine. Come on, Mary, you can be one of us," Steph coaxed.

Dread filled Mary. She felt like her body was being crushed. If she didn't get out of there, she felt like she would die. Mary turned to run. Surprisingly, the boys behind her let her go. The beat of her steps broke the silence of the woods. In the distance, she could here kids shouting. Above them all, Steph's voice was clearly audible . . .

"Worship the beast giving its life for us. Drink the blood that gives us power. All hail! All hail!"

The evil praises grew as Mary sprinted through the woods. She had no idea where she was. The only thing that mattered now was getting away from the crowd. The cold made her chest hurt. Scrambling into a large area of thick brush, Mary scanned the terrain to see if she'd been followed. Convinced that the coast was clear, she collapsed at the base of a tree. Sitting with her back against the trunk, she caught her breath and tried to get her bearings.

"Jesus, help me. Let me find my way home. Please!" Mary breathed.

The clouds parted. The moon came out lighting up the area. In the distance, she could make out the tall chimney of old Potts house. She knew her way home from here.

⁂

MARY STUMBLED TOWARD the back door of her house. It was late, but the lights were still on. That meant her parents knew she wasn't in her room.

"Busted," Mary said to herself. This might be a good busted. Maybe this was her chance to come clean with her parents. Two hours ago she was sprinting away from Steph and her followers. Now she was filthy. Her lip continued to bleed from a fall.

Feeling beaten and bruised, Mary just wanted to be five again so she could crawl up into her daddy's lap and have him wrap his arms around her. Life was so safe then. But she was not five. And telling her parents meant coming clean about everything . . . the tarot reading, her magic wand, and the Wiccan ceremony at Potts. She felt nauseous. *What would her dad do? How would he react? Would he love her anymore?* She had to tell him, even if it hurt them both.

Mary's trembling hand reached for the handle.

### DEWITCHING WITCHCRAFT

## HOLIDAYS IN THE OLD RELIGION

The journey to understanding the holidays that modern Wiccans celebrate is a journey back to the Old Religion. We'll start there and work our way through the Celts and forward to today.

The Old Religion was based heavily on agriculture. Ancient humanity's trust in the Mother Goddess who ruled the earth and the planting seasons led them to create a worship system based on the agricultural seasons. Wiccan scholars believe that ancient humanity created festivals, rituals, and worship around their planting and harvesting seasons, with major celebrations occurring at the beginning of each season.

Fast forward to the Celts, who also relied, in part, on agriculture. They combined the planting celebrations of the Old Religion with their own beliefs to create a religious system that was both tied to and dependent on these celebrations.

Their religious/agriculture system was fairly simple. Celts (like those of the Old Religion) believed that the world was originally divided into two parts. During the summer months when things grew, they believed that the goddess controlled the world and caused things to grow. During the winter months, the Celts believed that the dominant god was the male god of hunting and death. These beliefs dictated the Celtic celebration schedule. Major festivals were held at the change from the winter to the summer again when the season changed back to winter.

The festival held at the change from the summer and fall was called Samhain, and the festival held at the change from the winter to the summer was called Beltane. These major holidays were called Sabbats, which means to "celebrate" or "play." In addition to these two major Sabbats, the Celts added two others at the midpoint between these two seasonal changeovers. The one in the winter season was called Imbolic. The one in the summer was called Lughnasadh. These celebrations became known as the Four Major Sabbats, and today, while the exact dates for these vary by a few days depending on the different traditions, they are still celebrated in all Wiccan covens. They fall on our calendars in the following way.

## SAMHAIN (OCTOBER 31)

Samhain begins the Wiccan New Year, and is their most important celebration. This is the time of the year when they believe that the door to the world of the dead is open, and believers can talk with dead relatives.

*The history of how the Celtic Samhain become the Halloween we know today is found in the history of Pope Boniface IV. Around 609 AD he created All Saints Day, where Christians remember and venerate dead saints. Originally, this day was celebrated on May 13. However, in time it was moved to match with the Celtic Samhain, and the name changed from All Saints Day to All Hallows Day, and eventually became Halloween.*

## IMBOLIC (JANUARY 31)

This is the season between winter and spring. It's believed that spring is welling up in the belly of the mother goddess; therefore Wiccans honor her at this festival. This is the season where Wiccans purify themselves, and remove unhealthy habits and practices.

> *The Christian season of Lent begins just after the Wiccan season of Imbolic. Many Wiccans claim that the church adopted Imbolic's theme of purity into their Lent/Easter season.*

## BELTANE (APRIL 30)

Beltane marks the beginning of the light's half of the year, and the time when the mother goddess is emphasized. Beltane begins at the beginning of the second half of the year. The significance of fertility is highlighted. In Wiccan history, this is the time of the year when couples would connect sexually.

## LUGHNASADH (JULY 31)

Traditionally, this is a harvest festival and a celebration to the god Lugh, who was both a warrior and an athlete. Athletic games are often held in his honor.

> *When churches hold Harvest Festivals instead of Halloween Celebrations they're actually participating in another popular Wiccan celebration. The original purpose (in the Old Religion) was to celebrate the harvesting and planting seasons, which were thought to be connected to the mother/father gods. The practice continued to be carried through to Wicca today.*

To these four major Sabbats, the Celts added celebrations at the midpoints of each of the four quarters that coincide with the major seasonal changes (matching the placements of the sun). These are often referred to as the Four Minor Sabbats.

## YULE (DECEMBER 21, WINTER SOLSTICE)

Yule marks the time when the mother goddess gives birth to a new sun god. It's the time when Wiccans celebrate the renewal of life and rebirth. Tradition holds that Wiccans, with their reverence for spirits in trees, would decorate evergreen trees in celebration for the new life and renewal. Later, this practice became accepted by Christians and people of all faiths with the decoration of Christmas trees.

## OSTARA (SPRING EQUINOX)

Traditionally, Ostara marks the time of the year when Wiccans believe the mother goddess comes back from the underworld from her time of rest. Some Wiccans attempt to make a connection between the name Ostara and Easter, to unite this Wiccan day of celebration and Christianity's Easter. Many Wiccans note that the return of the mother goddess is much like the return of Christ after his death.

## LITHIA (JUNE 21, SUMMER SOLSTICE)

Lithia marks the beginning of the summer months when the days are longer. This celebration is thought to have been adopted possibly at a later date, thus not holding much historical significance.

## MABON (SEPTEMBER 21, AUTUMN EQUINOX)

Often thought of as the first day of fall, and the time when the Mother Goddess goes back into the underworld for rest.

All eight of these Sabbats were organized into the Wheel of the Year. This wheel is important to know and understand in order to grasp the Celtic and ancient mindset regarding these Sabbats. Below is an example of how the Wheel of the Year looked to the Celts, and possibly to other, older thinkers.

*One of the most important events Wiccans and Satanists celebrate is the cycle of the moon. New moons, and other moon cycles signify powerful moments where the spirit world is especially susceptible to magical manipulation.*

The wheel of the year reveals much about the ancient mindset, and even how modern Wiccans view the world. Life moves in a cyclical motion. Each season feeds the next season. All of this creates an understanding of the world that is woven together by events that go deeper than seasons. Originally, Wiccans thought the first half of the year was ruled by the mother goddess, and the second half ruled by the horned god. But today, with each passing season the worship and focus of the gods switch. Some seasons the mother is worshiped and revered. Other months, the father/horned god is revered. The changing of the seasons marks the changing of the focus of the worship.

## WHAT HAPPENS AT CELEBRATIONS

It's important to remember that tradition often changes with each generation, and this goes for many Wiccan celebrations today. In earlier times, Celts and Pagans held to strict religious celebrations. Since they were dependent on the earth and relied on the regularity of the seasons, their worship and celebrations at these times were an integral part of society. Today, celebrations (especially at the Sabbats) are more ceremonial and deserved simply out of tradition. By worshiping and celebrating many of these days, there's a connection to the ancient history of the religion and to the earliest ancestors who walked the path of the Old Religion.

Much of the current Wiccan worship is contextualized according to the coven, or person who is celebrating. Thus, Wiccans can celebrate anything anyway they want. However, in general, some of the ways they celebrate are below.

> When Wiccans celebrate at Sabbats, and include invocations and appeals to the mother/father gods, they are participating in the ancient form of sympathetic magic.

*Sabbat Celebration.* Sabbat celebrations can consist of a variety of events. There can be feasting, chanting, invocations to certain gods, prayers, etc. Depending on the season, different rituals can be performed. For example, at a Samhain Sabbat, coven members might perform acts of divination to connect with dead relatives. At a Mabon Sabbat, a coven might perform a ritual to welcome the Mother Goddess back to the surface of the earth.

*Dedication ceremonies.* Wiccans hold celebrations when someone becomes a member of their coven. At these ceremonies, the entire coven unites to dedicate the new member both to the coven and to the gods. There's also a celebration of the new member.

*Handfasting.* The Wiccan wedding ceremony is called Handfasting. Witches getting married in this manner exchange rings, vows, and are married by a Wiccan priest. Wiccan marriages typically last for as long as their love lasts, and they're encouraged to not continue their relationship after their love for each other has ended. When their love is over, Wiccan couples can participate in ceremonies or rituals called Parting of the Ways or Handparting, which are equal to a divorce.

*Wiccaning.* When a child is dedicated to the Wiccan craft by their parents, they go through a Wiccaning ceremony. This is a lot like the Christian form of baptism or dedication where the church recognizes the child is dedicated to God. Wiccans dedicate their children to the gods in a ritual that includes incense and prayers. Children who go through the Wiccaning ceremony aren't required to follow Wicca their entire lives. The ceremony only dedicates them until a time when the child is old enough to make a choice about their spiritual path.

> *The desire to celebrate at religious festivals is obviously built into the human psyche. Even without recognizing God, Wiccans have created a series of festivals and celebrations that include the worship of their deities. What does it say about the way humans are made that we have this inborn desire? Why are we built to praise something other than ourselves?*

## SATANIC CELEBRATIONS

Satanism is a personal religion. Adherents can create their own beliefs, their own celebrations, their own rituals, and their own holidays. Additionally, many of the satanic holidays fall on the same days as the Wiccan holidays, making another interesting connection between these two "different" religions.

What Satanists do on celebration days depends somewhat on the group or solitary Satanist. They (like Wiccans) can hold a special celebration like a worship service. There are also private, more personal ways to celebrate.

Usually, Satanists will hold special worship services aimed at celebrating the holiday. They'll perform magic, perform a sex ritual, or worship (themselves, humanity, or the god "Satan") in groups or alone.

It's important to remember that Satanists do not hold to particular dates and traditions in their celebration of satanic holidays. Satanism is a highly personal religion with adherents always revising and reinventing the religion. New holidays and new ways to celebrate show up often.

## SATANIC HOLIDAYS

The satanic church celebrates a variety of holidays. In one sense, the distinctiveness of Satanism lends itself to celebrating the same holidays as Wicca, but in unique ways. In another, Satanism doesn't do anything more unique than Wicca. Satanism, like Wicca, takes solstices and holidays, ties them into their belief about the universe, and creates worship and celebrations out of that combination. Some of the specific days of celebration follow:

*Birthdays.* Satanism is a selfish religion. It is self-focused. It is self-serving. This is in keeping with Anton LaVey's original teachings, and much of the current teachings of the church and the various offshoots of the church. There is no single ritual that all Satanists use to celebrate a birthday, it is held as the most important day of the year for the Satanist.

*Solstices.* Satanists (like Wiccans) hold celebrations based on the movement of the sun. Like Wicca, Satanists celebrate the spring and autumn equinox, and the summer and winter solstice. These solstices are thought of as perfect days to make a change in one's life.

*Planting Dates.* Satanists don't call them *planting* dates, and don't adhere to the agricultural theme. Yet, they still worship on the dates that Wiccans do, even if not for the same reason.

*Why do these specific dates and holidays show up in both Wicca and Satanism? What is the significance that both of these religions use the same dates, but emphasize different meanings of these events?*

The manner of celebrating on holidays is one of the most notable differences between Wicca and Satanism. Wicca often seems "tamer," maybe even "less dangerous," than the harsh and dangerous beliefs of Satanism. This theme continues in their celebration of holidays, and in the differences of how they celebrate. Consider:

*Beltane.* In Wicca, Beltane marks the emergence of the mother goddess, and the idea of fertility and sexuality are encouraged and emphasized. In Satanism, this day is taken to the extreme and celebrated as a day of lust and indulgence. It's one of Satanism's most holy days, and usually called Walpurgisnacht.

*Samhain.* In Wicca, this is the beginning of the year. It's an important day in Wicca, when followers believe they can contact their dead relatives. In Satanism, Samhain is a time to perform destruction rituals and get revenge on others.

## CHRISTIAN HOLIDAYS

Some historians, scholars, philosophers, and religious leaders argue either that Christian holidays were adopted from early Pagan beliefs, or that Christian holidays are older than Pagan holidays or come from different roots than Pagan holidays. It's not the purpose of this chapter to prove or disprove a relationship between the dates for Christian holidays and Pagan holidays. However, with the numerous similarities between Christian holidays and the celebration dates in Wicca and Satanism, one has to wonder what these similarities really mean.

> *Some scholars argue that the church chose to celebrate Christian holidays on the same dates as important Pagan holidays to make Christianity more acceptable to the Pagans.*

Many of the exact dates Christians celebrate as holidays are still debated by scholars—including the birth and resurrection of Jesus. The importance of Christian holidays is the emphasis placed on the day by believers. We know that Jesus was born, and we choose to celebrate his birth on December 25th. We recognize his death and resurrection in the spring because we celebrate the price Jesus paid for us. The emphasis isn't on the date, but on the *event*. It's interesting that many Christian celebration dates fall on important dates from Pagan, Wiccan, satanic, Celtic and other religions and cultures. Beyond that fact, it's the meaning of the event that's important.

Christians today don't celebrate planting seasons or equinoxes because our religion isn't earth based. We don't celebrate these things because the focus and basis of our belief is neither grounded in this world nor based on the order of this world.

*Of all the Christian holy days, Easter is the one that some non-Christian religious groups try to own. Wiccan scholars often cite the rebirth and renewal theme in their religion as the original Easter and the origin of the "myth" of the resurrection of Jesus. However, aside from the fact that the resurrection actually happened, it is actually one date that hasn't been moved throughout history. Jesus entered Jerusalem to celebrate the Passover; he was tried, crucified, buried, and resurrected a few days after Passover. These are specific dates in history that have not changed.*

Celebration is the essence of community. Celebration is what binds people together into community. In the next chapter, we'll get a deeper understanding of how Wiccans and Satanists organize themselves, how others become members in their groups, and what is expected of their members.

# Chapter 11

# ON THE ROPES
*Covens*

C4's parent meetings were usually boring. Mitch always began with prayer and quoted the RealWalk vision. He didn't want parents to forget the purpose for the ministry.

Tonight, after the introduction, Mitch launched into a PowerPoint presentation of the recent youth retreat. Pictures of packed buses, smiling kids, Mitch speaking, kids praying, the volleyball tournament, and small group circles flashed across the wall. Upbeat Christian music played in the background. The final slide thanked the parents for their prayers and support.

When the lights came back on, Mitch looked out at the smiling parents. He could tell that they were pleased to see their children in the pictures.

"I think the most important thing I ought to mention about our youth retreat was the subject matter. With the approach of Halloween, I decided that we should study its origins. So we've been talking about witchcraft during our weekly RealWalk meetings. I used the retreat as an opportunity to really drive home the evils of witchcraft and satanic worship. I've been giving them some of the background of witchcraft. We've discussed very generally about how witches worship, how they cast spells and how it stands in direct contrast with biblical teaching. I feel that this is a very timely study based on what's been happening in our city lately."

Bob Farley always disagreed with Mitch. Mitch could teach kids about the love of Christ, and Bob would level some charge against him. Tonight was no different. "Hold on, Mitch. I'm concerned about what you're teaching. It's okay to tell kids about spiritual warfare, but you're giving them too much information. I'm afraid that some kids will be lured into practicing witchcraft because of the information you've given them. You're not being careful enough."

"I'm not saying it's okay to do it. I'm telling them how dangerous all of this is. If a student gets involved in these practices, it's not because of anything I've said here. Besides, many of them already know a lot about witchcraft. Look, five minutes on the Internet and your kids will know more than what I've taught." Mitch was obviously trying to keep his tone steady and his emotions in check. But it was difficult. He was convinced that the kids who came to C4's RealWalk needed to hear this.

Marcie was Chief Collins' wife and Shelby's mother. Marcie jumped in to support Mitch. "I'm with Mitch on this one. The media constantly bombards our kids with this information. All you have to do is listen to the radio. Those cow mutilations are happening more and more. They need to be aware of the dangers of these practices and be given a biblical perspective. Besides, it's up to us as parents to know what our kids are into. We can't lay the raising of our kids on Mitch's shoulders."

Shelby joined her mom in support of Mitch. "You guys don't realize how much we already know. Kids talk about this stuff all the time at school. And the whole cow thing has made a lot of us afraid. We don't . . ."

Farley interrupted Shelby. "They're cows, not people. Unless you know more than we do, the police have yet to determine the motives behind these slaughters. It's probably a bunch of teenagers out for a thrill, or maybe a deranged homeless person wanting food. It's a little far fetched to say that a bunch of witches living in Clarke City are responsible for this. You're putting fear into a bunch of impressionable children, Mitch."

Pastor Rick walked in and sat at the back with his wife in the middle of Bob's response.

Relieved to see Pastor Rick, Mitch boldly said, "The thing we have to realize is that Christians aren't the only ones living in Clarke City. It just stands to reason that among the various religious beliefs practiced here, witchcraft is among them. Our students need to understand why Christianity is the only true religion. The Bible explains that we are in a spiritual battle, and your kids are right in the middle whether you want them to be or not."

"There is no battle, Mitch, except for the one you've created," Farley continued. "If our kids are in the middle, it's because you've placed them there. You've taken this too far."

At this point, Pastor Rick stood to talk. This made Mitch feel good. He knew that Rick would support him. He'd always backed him up in the past.

"I hate to say this, Mitch, but I think you've gone a little too far too. You have to realize that other religions are able to exist in harmony. The more you teach on this, the more you promote hatred. Our God is not one of hatred, but of love. To teach otherwise is theologically incorrect. That is when the fight begins."

One at a time, parents began nodding their heads in agreement with Rick. Some hadn't thought of it that way before, but it made sense. Seeing the agreement spread across the room, Rick came to the front where Mitch was standing. He leaned in to whisper in Mitch's ear, "Be careful that you know your audience before you preach against us." Mitch's face turned white.

Placing his hand on Mitch's shoulder, Rick turned to face the parents. "Folks, obviously, Mitch is capable of presenting a quality youth program and the students love him. However, his lack of discretion in his teaching troubles me as much as it does you. I promise you that from now on I'll be consulting with Mitch about the content of RealWalk. We'll get this cleared up in no time."

Rick closed with a short prayer. Most parents avoided eye contact with Mitch as they filed out. The few who did look at him just shook their heads. Bob shook Rick's hand and said, "Thanks, Rick, for stepping in when you did. I don't know what it is about Mitch, but he always seems to pick a fight with me. And tonight he had parents ganging up on me too. It was starting to get really ugly and my ulcer can't stand all this tension. I really appreciate you, Rick. You truly know how to bring peace to a situation."

⚜

SOFT, INSTRUMENTAL CHRISTIAN music oozed soothingly from the stereo in Mitch's office. His head was in his hands. Tears gently dropped onto the desk in front of him. Mitch was beat up and bruised emotionally. He felt like he was bleeding to death on the battlefield with no one around to help him. The one person who was supposed to watch his back stuck a knife in it instead.

"Jesus, help me!" he moaned. "I know that you called me here to this church for this work. Why did you let this happen? What did I do wrong? What's going on?"

Just then, there was a knock at his office door. Pastor Rick walked in and sat in one of two empty chairs on the other side of Mitch's desk.

"Thanks a lot, Rick," Mitch said wiping his eyes. "I've spent years building up credibility with these parents. And in one night, you destroyed everything. Why did you do that to me?"

"Don't raise your voice to me, Mitch. You are the one in the wrong here, not me. Everyone saw that tonight. I was polite before because we were in front of people. Now, I'm just going to be honest. You're creating a disruption here. You have become divisive."

Mitch quickly reached for his Bible. Scriptures leapt into his head about teaching the truth, standing against Satan, knowing the difference between truth and lies. Maybe if he could show Rick some of the things he'd been teaching, he'd understand that Mitch was not in the wrong.

Rick leapt to his feet. "Do *not* do that." Rick leaned across Mitch's desk. Inches from his face, Rick seethed, "Don't you thump the Bible at me. Look at you, all convinced about your truth, *your* belief. You never stop to consider that others might believe differently. You don't have one tolerant bone in your body, Mitch. That's been your problem since you started here."

Rick was standing so close that it was impossible for Mitch to thumb his way through his Bible without backing away.

"You're a disappointment," Rick said, sneering in Mitch's face.

A volleyball-sized lump formed in Mitch's throat. He felt nine years old again, being punished for having a messy room.

"You're an embarrassment," Rick continued, "trying to impress Chief Collins with all your 'knowledge.' Well, it didn't work did it? You're pathetic." Mitch began to feel heavy, like he'd just been saddled with a 200-pound body suit. His face burned. With each jab, a wave of humiliation swept over him. Flashbacks of his father screaming at him rolled through his mind. His shoulders slumped. This was a battle Rick was winning.

"You could get fired, with no severance pay. You'd have to move out of the parsonage and I know you don't have any savings. You'll be homeless . . . you and that nice family of yours. Then, you'll be worthless to them too." Rick's oily words slid out of his mouth.

The ringing phone interrupted the fight. It was the church's private line.

"What's up, honey," Mitch asked, visibly shaken.

"Mitch, can you come home? I'm scared."

"Scared? Baby, what's wrong?" Rick heard this. He smiled.

"I was cleaning up the living room and all of a sudden I felt like

I was going to die. There was a heaviness. I . . . I can't explain it, Mitch. But I'm scared. I need you home. Now."

Mitch hung up the phone and looked at Rick, who had settled into the chair. He looked like he was planning to stay. The smug look on his face told a story Mitch didn't have time to unravel.

"Everything okay at home, Mitch?" Rick drawled.

"No, I need to go. We'll have to finish this later," Mitch said, walking toward the door.

Rick blocked his path. "Mitch, I think you need time to think things over. Take a few days off. Get your spiritual life together. Reconnect with that beautiful family of yours." Rick's words rang with pride, like he'd just netted a huge fish. "When you get back, we'll talk about our new plan for RealWalk and your new accountability group. Farley says he has an opening in his. I think it'd be good for you."

Mitch looked at Rick incredulously. "Do you have a problem with that?" Rick asked.

Mitch swallowed and shook his head. He pushed past Rick and sprinted down the hall.

"Many paths, Mitch," Rick shouted. There was glee in his voice. "You have to respect all paths. Remember your beautiful family, Mitch."

DEWITCHING WITCHCRAFT

Wicca and Satanism are vastly different in how they organize in groups. Wicca relies on a looser organizational style. However, churches that worship Satan are more organized and follow a chain of command that stretches from the leader of the organization, down to the leadership of each local group.

## WICCAN ORGANIZATION

We've seen that Wicca has specific beliefs about how the universe operates, how magic happens, etc. Interestingly enough, the area of community organization is one area where Wicca does not take a specific stand. There are no rule books about how groups of Wiccans are to conduct themselves. There is no organizing group of witches that oversees the conduct its members. You cannot go to any city in any place in the United States and find the First Church of Wicca. There is not a group who serves all Wiccan believers in any legal, religious or professional way.

> *The one exception to the "No Wiccan Organization" theory is the Council of American Witches, which existed for a short time beginning in 1973. The council attempted to unite Wiccans and bring some kind of cohesive feeling to the practice of witchcraft. However, because of Wicca's independent nature, the council disbanded shortly after it was organized.[1]*

However, witches do attempt to organize themselves, despite their independence and lack of global accountability.

## COVENS

The only group organization that occurs in Wicca is in the area of covens. The idea of the Wiccan coven was unheard of until the witch trials began in Europe and America. According to Raymond Buckland, noted Wiccan historian and scholar, the word *coven* was first used in 1662 at the trial of a suspected witch named Issobel Gowdie. In that trial, the accused witch explained how her group got together and what they did when they met. She called her witch group a coven. Since then, the word has been used to denote a group of witches gathering together for celebration, ritual, and magic. Here are some specifics of what we know about covens:

## COVEN LEADERSHIP

Covens are led by a High Priest or Priestess who makes many of the decisions for the coven and leads in worship and ritual. Sometimes, the leadership includes a person in training to become a High Priestess, called a Maiden. Her training is for the purpose of eventually leading a coven on her own.

## NUMBER

The number of witches in a coven can vary. Traditionally, the number of witches in a coven is thirteen—twelve members with one leader (the High Priest or Priestess) However, there doesn't have to be thirteen in each coven. Within each coven there can also be an inner circle of members called *elders*. These elders are more advanced Wiccans who make leadership decisions for the coven.

## GROUP PRACTICES

Witches get together for a variety of reasons. Typically, covens get together to worship their god and goddess, as well as to practice magic and ritual, and celebrate a Sabbat. Covens usually gather at the home of their High Priest or Priestess.

## COVEN MEMBERSHIP

Becoming a member of a coven happens in a variety of ways. Some Wiccan teachers note that the best way to become a member of a coven is to get friends together who believe the same way you do, and start your own. Another is to be invited. Either way, going through the steps to becoming a member of a coven requires initiation through rituals that are usually specific to that coven. In the case of new covens, members either adopt rituals used in other covens, or they make up their own.

*Witches don't have to meet and practice in covens. A special name,* solitaries, *is given to witches who practice the craft alone. These witches prefer a more personalized and isolated practice and are supported in their craft by all Wiccan churches. Solitaries are considered official witches and have the same status, responsibility, and power as witches who practice within a coven.*

## DEGREES AND LEVELS OF MEMBERSHIP.

In some cases, covens are organized around levels of membership. These levels are called "degrees." Not all covens agree with this kind of membership. One popular form of Wicca, called Gardenian (named after Gerald Gardner), uses this degree system. Where members in the lowest level (first degree) are allowed to participate in some practices, but only as a spectator. A second-degree member is allowed to practice magic, and a third-degree member is allowed to start their own coven.[2]

## ORGANIZATION IN THE CHURCH OF SATAN

Unlike Wicca, most churches that worship Satan are organized in a specific way. There are articles of incorporation for each church, duties and responsibilities each church must abide by, and even a loose form of accountability to a leadership body that oversees (in a general way) all of the churches.

Like other churches, the church of Satan is incorporated. Like many different Christian denominations, the Church of Satan, including many of the different offshoots, is organized and has official stages of membership.

*Not everyone who worships Satan belongs to a satanic church. Many adherents worship Satan in their own way apart from any connection to the larger body of satanic believers.*

## THE MOTHER CHURCH

Depending on the branch of Satanism, there is one official church that governs and oversees the entire denomination. However, this varies depending on the branch of Satanism. We've already mentioned two official larger groups of organized Satanists—the Church of Satan (organized by Anton LaVey) and the Temple of Set (organized Michael Acquino, a student of LaVey). There are several other churches in America who believe in, and worship, Satan. These groups are organized much like any other church. They have a leadership council, head "pastors" (they're called priests in many of their churches), rules, etc. They're organized much like any other church in America, which is pretty interesting. Satanism is known for its rejection of Christianity, and its attempt to do everything backward. Yet, in organization and structure, they mirror the Christian church very closely.

> *The actual number of Satanists in America is often debated among satanic believers. Some Satanists claim that there are millions of Satanists in America including those who are members and nonmembers of churches. Others have said that their numbers are in the thousands.*

> *You don't have to be a member of a satanic church to be considered a follower of Satan. Many official satanic church documents stress that followers can practice on their own without an official church connection.*

## CHURCH MEMBERSHIP

Generally, church membership in any church of Satan occurs through a series of checking and observing. While anyone can become an apprentice in many satanic churches, membership at an advanced level requires that members have background checks, and be observed for their commitment to Satan, to other believers, and to the church. In some instances, members must be leaders in their community, have an acceptable financial history, own a home, and have a good job.

Each satanic church is different, and membership varies depending on the church. The following steps to full membership are from the Church of Satan.[3] The Temple of Set differs somewhat in the names it gives each level, and requires somewhat different levels of acceptance depending on the degree.

## THE FIRST DEGREE

This is the lowest level of membership. Members at this level agree with the basic philosophy of the Church of Satan. This is the level at which most people are members and requires little participation. One can be affiliated either as someone who practices within an officially recognized church, or as a solitary practitioner.

## SECOND DEGREE

Members who demonstrate an understanding of the basic satanic philosophy and portray a commitment to the church are awarded admittance to this degree. Members at this level are usually allowed to hold position of leadership within the local satanic church.

## THIRD DEGREE

Believers who complete requirements for satanic priesthood, undergo an evaluation and training, and who pass a strenuous background examination are allowed into this degree. People accepted into this degree are called priests or priestesses of Mendes.

## FOURTH DEGREE

As a member becomes more skilled at understanding Satanism, and leading within the church, they are awarded this degree. Typically, these members are upper-level leadership within the church.

They have demonstrated a complete giving of themselves to the cause of the church, and to Satan (whether Satan be literal or figurative).

## FIFTH DEGREE

This is the highest degree one can attain in the Church of Satan. It's also called the high priest. Throughout the history of the church it has been held by very few people. This position is also called "Magus 5" and is said to be decided on by Satan. While he was alive, Anton LaVey held this office.

*In Acts 8:9–25 Simon the Sorcerer is also called Simon Magus.*

## GENERAL CHURCH LEADERSHIP

The Church of Satan is led and directed by two main groups. The Council of Nine decides policy, offers membership to the advanced degrees, and directs the church. This council is made up of eight members, with the ninth being the "Magus 5" or high priest. The Order of the Trapezoid also presides over membership, and other administrative details.

## THE ORGANIZATION OF THE CHRISTIAN CHURCH

The Christian church has a long and interesting history. Scripture gives us a good description of what the early church was like by describing the conduct of the disciples and early believers after the resurrection and ascension of Jesus. We see Peter emerging as the first evangelical preacher, Paul coming forward as an effective missionary, and the first believers struggling to discover correct doctrine and conduct.

Acts offers us two glimpses into the corporate conduct of early believers. Acts 2:42–47 and Acts 4:32–35 describe these believers as a sharing, worshiping group who cared for the hurting in society. These believers had firsthand knowledge of the ministry of Jesus. After its early formation, the church organized various councils and gatherings to accomplish a number of tasks, including: Deciding correct doctrine; Verifying which writings, letters, and gospels were authentic and inspired; Thinking through difficult decisions, like requirements for pastor.; Issuing statements about specific hypocritical teachers.

Many of these began in the late 100s AD, and have continued to today. Through the years, the Christian church has separated into different denominations. Each has different meetings, different organizational structures, and believe somewhat differently about some Christian basics. However, groups of believers who accept the existence of God, the divinity and authority of Jesus, the inerrancy and authority of Scripture. and the teachings found in Scripture as being complete and unalterable *are* unified, despite minor doctrinal differences. In 1 Corinthians, Paul calls these believers the "body of Christ" (1 Corinthians 12:1–31). Later in Scripture, these believers are called the "Bride of Christ" (Revelations 21:1–4). Scripture teaches that one day, Jesus will return to claim his bride, and take her with him to live in a new place and enjoy unending fellowship with God (Revelations 21:9–22:6).

## THE BIGGEST DIFFERENCE

The difference between Christianity, Wiccan, and satanic organizations is in their goals. Wiccans organize to perform ritual and practice magic. Satanists organize to worship Satan. They seek to promote and further their beliefs. Both promote theories, ideas and practices that are anti-Christian. At times, their mission is more about telling people how wrong Christianity is, hoping to show hypocritical or fallen believers as examples of what all Christians are like. Other times, they offer overly positive or gentle images, telling only half-truths about their religion.

Scripture unites Christians around two central missions. In Mark 12:29–31, Jesus points out that the most important command any believer can live out is to love God, and love others. Jesus clearly states that above all other commands, rules, and expectations, these two are clearly the most important. Love is mission number one for the believer. Our love for God must be evident and clear. Our love for God must motivate us to love others (1 John 4:21). This love motivates us to our other mission—to tell others about the saving grace of Jesus Christ. This is commanded by Jesus to his disciples in Matthew 28:18–20.

These two aims—love and missions—are the biggest differences between Wicca, Satanism, and Christianity. Christians focus their love on the one, true God, the God who is above Wicca, Satanism, and all religions, and they use that love as their motivator to tell others about Jesus Christ, who is the non-believer's only hope for eternity.

# NIGHT FLIGHT
## *The Wicca-Satan Connection*

ary took a deep breath and turned the handle, but suddenly the door flung open. She jumped back. Her dad stood there with bags in his hands. He didn't look up as he headed for the car.

"Where have *you* been?"

Mary braced for the onslaught from her dad as her mom walked out and locked the door. She looked scared.

"What's going on, Mom? Why are we leaving?" Mary's legs felt like Jell-O.

Over her shoulder she said, "Go ahead and get in the car, sweetie. We'll explain on the way."

&&&

MITCH, SANDY, AND Mary drove through the country. The cool night air was a gift. With the windows down, no one felt the pressure to talk. The only sound in the McCorkle car was the sound of the wind rushing through their car. The road was as empty as their hearts. Clouds covered the light of the moon. It was an eerie, desperate night—the perfect night to escape Clarke City.

Mitch stared blankly at the road. *What do I say to Mary?* Mitch thought to himself. *Honey, your father is a failure . . . not spiritual enough.* His mind replayed a series of opportunities he had missed with his daughter and chosen, instead, to spend with the broken kids of Clarke City. He was doubly defeated, spiritually disemboweled. *Someone* is *winning,* Mitch thought, *and it's not me.*

Mary sat in the back seat letting the wind whip her hair around. She wondered when her parents would tell her what was going on. She could see her dad's face in the rearview mirror. His forehead was wrinkled with sadness; his eyes, swollen. Did they know where she had been? What she'd been through? Is that why they were so upset? Mary felt sick. She knew she had to confess everything. She had to set the record straight. This could ruin things, but it was her only hope of not being abandoned by her parents. Suddenly, the McCorkle's compact car felt huge. The gulf between Mitch and Mary had become endless. Bottomless. Impassible.

In the rearview mirror, Mitch looked at the beautiful face of his daughter that he'd loved since her birth. He could still smell the sweetness of her new skin, just hours old. He recalled her first smile, her first steps, the first time she said "Daddy." He remembered countless times he told her bedtime stories tucking her in afterward. "You are my masterpiece," he would say with a confident smile, kissing her good night. Life was sweet back then. Where had the time gone? Who was this troubled young woman in the backseat?

Tears began to stream down Mitch's face. Mary curled up in the backseat and tried to hold back the sobs. Sandy reached for her husband's hand. The experience in Clarke City had tested their small family. It had tested their understanding of God.

Mitch pulled the car into a hotel parking lot. "I'll go in and see if they have any rooms. Hang tight. I'll be right back," he said, wiping his eyes and cheeks. Sandy noticed for the first time Mary's swollen lip and her dirty clothes.

"Mary!" she exclaimed, horrified by what she saw. "What happened?"

Mary couldn't hold it back any longer as the sobs racked her body. Sandy quickly scrambled into the backseat and held her weeping daughter.

Mitch dropped his credit card on the counter of the Country Motor Lodge. The price of the room didn't matter. Cable, complimentary coffee, heated pool . . . it was the farthest thing from his mind. A safe room was all he wanted. He grabbed the room keys and headed back to the car.

"What's wrong?" Mitch said, sticking his head through the open car window.

"I don't know yet. She hasn't been able to speak. Let's just get in the room and get this all sorted out."

The room was small, and packed with tired furniture. Mitch dropped the bags on the old knee-high dresser and turned to the bed where his wife sat holding their daughter. Something had happened to Mary.

Kneeling in front of his daughter, Mitch tenderly said, "Tell me what happened, sweetheart."

Mary buried her head in Mitch's chest and sobbed. Now secure in her parents' love, the whole awful story poured out.

The McCorkles spent the night holding each other, confessing, and asking forgiveness. As the sky was beginning to turn gray with the first light of day, the hurting family fell asleep, emotionally and physically exhausted.

They were far from being okay, but they were headed in the right direction.

## DEWITCHING WITCHCRAFT

## THE GENERAL RELIGIOUS CONNECTION

Ninian Smart notes in his book *The Religious Experience of Mankind* that there are similarities in all religions. Every religious belief system has themes or topics that it attempts to address. In his book, he unravels some of these similarities between Wicca and Satanism. One of Smart's first statements in his book (and one point that he seems to bring up throughout the book) is that human society always has a religious element. Religion—both religious beliefs and religious practices—forms much of the foundation for society and for smaller communities within that society. Religion has existed since the dawn of humanity as an ongoing attempt to explain origins and order. It has existed to demonstrate that humanity has both a purpose and a destination. The fact that societies always have some form of religious element points to the immediate natural connection between Wicca and Satanism. They're both religions within a society. They're both natural developments by humans to offer answers to some basic questions of humanity.

Among Smart's excellent treatments of some of the basic beliefs of many popular religions, he notes that the following dimensions exist in all religions. I've listed the dimensions below, with a short sentence or two of my own for explanation.

## THE RITUAL DIMENSION

All people who involve themselves in religious belief and practice organize themselves around and participate in ritual. Certain prayers and invocations can become rituals. Ritual isn't concerned so much with the unseen world as it is with gathering people together around specific practices.

## THE MYTHOLOGICAL DIMENSION

Smart uses the word *myth* to denote the idea of story. Every religious group has their own "myth" or "story" that they rely on to describe the origin or nature of things. An example of the use of story is Genesis 1:1–26. This story includes how the world came into existence, and the creation of humanity.

## THE DOCTRINAL DIMENSION

Doctrine is the attempt to give myth a rational basis. Doctrine is the theological belief that every religious system has. While doctrine is based in the rational, it relies on the stories of the religion to give the doctrine or theology historical roots.

## THE ETHICAL DIMENSION

Ethics, rules of conduct for the adherents of the system, exist in all religious belief. In fact, Smart notes, that ethics exist both within and outside religious belief. Ethics build religious belief, but they also build structures that societies are based on. Religious systems have most often formed the ethical structures on which most societies are based.

## THE SOCIAL DIMENSION

Religion invites adherents into more than a system of belief. It invites believers to a social structure based, in part, on the ethical, doctrinal and mythological assumptions within the religion. This social dimension includes the involvement of priests or religious leaders as part of that social structure. It's the social structure that maintains and governs the community, and its adherents. At some level, religious structures fulfill more than ethical or doctrinal needs, and fill social needs as well.

## The Experiential Dimension

Religious belief is based upon the hope that humans can have an experience with another realm—whether that realm is the divine, unseen, or whatever. Smart notes that it's this element that sometimes makes some religious systems seem non-religious. They are religious but without the expectation of an experience with another realm (like some Satanists).

Following Smart's thinking for a moment, we realize that all religions have similar elements. We learn that all religions have a ritualistic element. All religions use myth and story to explain their beliefs and origins. All form doctrinal statements and positions to explain the theological meaning within their religion.

I point out Smart's thinking here to try and take away some of the common footholds many Christians use to climb what I consider to be tall places around Wicca and Satanism so they can throw stones. So often, when you listen to much of what Christians have to say to Wiccans and Satanists about their religions, they appear to be throwing paper wads at a charging tiger. Many of their proofs against Wiccans and Satanists are silly, overemotional, and ineffective. Christians sometimes take issue with Wiccan ritual when in fact all religions use ritual. They take issue with magic when all religions have some method of contacting the divine on behalf of humanity. On this level, Wicca, Satanism, and Christianity are very similar.

However, on another level, there are connections between these beliefs that are impossible to ignore. These connections go to a deeper level than just the spiritual elements similar in all religions. These qualities are unique to these two belief systems that claim independence in thought and origin.

## The Brotherhood of Satan

Ultimately, all religions that deny the Lordship of Jesus Christ, the existence of God and his revealed nature in Scripture and the existence and workings of the Holy Spirit in the natural and spiritual world are wrong. Every belief that doesn't align itself with Scripture is wrong. Every belief. No matter what they do, how kind their actions how pleasant their adherents, or how good their intentions.

Obviously, evangelical Christians believe that at a very deep level, Satanism is not in any way consistent with Christianity. The story of Satan begins in the Garden of Eden. There, Satan revealed that he had the crafty ability to twist truth so that humans would deny God's laws. In the New Testament the entire realm of Satan was exposed, introducing hell, demons, and spiritual forces, all of which war against Christians seeking to twist truth and relationships, and trick people into stumbling in their walk with God. From the story of Eden, through history, and to this moment, God's adversary has consistently appeared in keeping with his revealed nature in Scripture.

With Satanism being the oldest non-Christian religion existing in society, Wicca has to be its sibling, dependent on it for its philosophy and ideology. Therefore, to accurately view Satanism and Wicca requires realizing that, when we see these religions, we're looking at them through specific lenses or preconceived notions that we hold about these religions.

Christians view Satan and the worship of Satan through the lens of Scripture. We know what to think about Satan from the biblical descriptions of who Satan is and what his purpose is. We know about the war that Christians face as they seek to oppose the work Satan is doing on Earth. Wicca has to be viewed through our understanding of what Satanism is as described in Scripture. Because Satanism is older than Wicca and the primary anti-God religion, Wicca has borrowed many elements from it. The only way we can effectively understand what Wicca is and how destructive it can be is to also look at Satanism, its close philosophical sibling.

When you consider the primacy of the existence of Satan along with the numerous similarities between these two beliefs, the dangers of Wicca become impossible to ignore. Wicca no longer appears as a kind, gentle, earth-based religion, or as a quiet attempt to worship an unnamed god. Instead, Wicca becomes a scary religion interwoven with satanic thought, ideas, principles, and practices. It becomes a religion tightly mixed with satanic symbols. It becomes a religion darkened by the belief in unseen powers and spirits living in kinship with satanic thought and principles, when fully mixed into the system causes destruction and death.

And this, interestingly enough, is the singular most interesting difference between these two religions. Wicca, borrowing many satanic principles, beliefs, ideas, and philosophy, is an easier religion to adopt than Satanism. However, it's clearly a close relative to Satanism. The craftiness of Satan hasn't stopped. He remains, using the same deceptive principles he has used throughout the centuries, as far back as the Garden of Eden. He deceptively hides in Wicca, an easier to accept, popular form of Satanism.

Christians today aren't the only people who have faced witchcraft and Satanism. The Bible is dripping with evidence that believers encountered many forms of Witchcraft. What were these? How did believers handle them? What specifically does God's Word say about what witchcraft is and how you should handle it? In the next chapter, we'll dive into the biblical understanding of witchcraft, and learn how we should deal with it.

## THE BIG DATE

*The Bible and Witchcraft*

*J*ared was excited. He fidgeted in his seat waiting for the final bell. He had waited for this night for a long time. In just a few short hours, he would be picking Steph up at her house for dinner and Putt-Putt.

The bell finally rang. Jared sprinted to his locker. He had to get home quickly. He still had to take a shower and fix his hair. It took a long time and a lot of gel to achieve that tousled look.

"Jared!" Paul dialed the combination to his locker.

"Bro. Tonight is *the* night!"

"Go, man! Go!"

"Later," Jared yelled, half way down the hall.

Jared burst through the school doors and headed toward the parking lot. No time to care what Paul was up to. No time to look for Mary. . . . Where was she? No worries about Shelby's strange new beliefs, either. Tonight would be a night to remember. Jared was sure of it.

⁂

MITCH WALKED TOWARD Rick's office resigned to work with him. He and his family had spent the last few days holed up in the

Motor Lodge doing a lot of soul searching. With their family relationship on the mend, Mitch had to decide what to do about his ministry. After several hours of prayer, asking for clear direction from the Lord, he still didn't feel free to leave C4. Maybe he could back off of his "in your face" style, but he wouldn't compromise the truth. He hoped that he and Rick could come to middle ground.

Mitch knocked on Rick's door and heard, "Come in." Opening the door, he was surprised by what he saw. Around the room sat the elders of C4: Bob Farley; Jerry Poulson, a successful plastic surgeon; Willie Banks, the church's attorney; and Frank Miller, Rick's brother-in-law. These men were the core leadership of C4. In the center of the semi-circle of elders sat Pastor Rick, notepad in his lap, looking at Mitch over the top of his bifocals.

"Oh, I'm sorry. I didn't know you were busy," Mitch said, backing out of the room. "I'll come back later, Rick."

"Wait a minute, Mitch. We're actually discussing you. You might as well stay," Rick said.

Mitch felt sick. He didn't trust these men. Alone, each of these men could be an encouraging bunch. Together, they could be vicious.

"We're concerned about you, Mitch. After last week's parents' meeting, you and your family disappeared without a trace. Where have you been?" Rick's pointed question took Mitch by surprise.

"I was just doing what you told me to do, Rick. I got away for a few days," Mitch answered.

"I *never* told you to do that. I told you to take a few days and re-think your position on teaching intolerance. I never told you to leave town and not tell anyone where you were going!" Rick's response was calculated.

Mitch sat red faced and speechless. Did he not hear Rick correctly that night?

"Mitch, we're meeting because we care about you and the youth ministry," Bob Farley began. "You've taught some things that have caused the parents of C4 to lose confidence in you. And your little disappearing act has caused us to lose confidence in you, too."

Mitch expected an attack from Bob, but the presence of the other elders made Bob's words sting. "Bob, if you'll tell me who is talking I can go to them and we can talk about what's bothering them. I want to be able to help parents feel comfortable with . . ."

"The parents don't want to talk to you, Mitch. They've come to us in confidence because they're afraid of you. And we will not betray that confidence!"

Jerry Paulson jumped in. "Mitch, the parents of this church can be fierce. Once you've done something questionable, they're slow to forgive. They're tough people. Overprotective."

Mitch's head was swimming. *What were they saying?* His eyes caught Rick's, who was staring at Mitch. "Mitch, we'd like for you to submit your resignation. This is for your own protection. C4 has become harmful to you and your family."

Mitch sat in the huge leather chair. Numbness spread over his body. He was speechless. He looked from face to face trying to comprehend what was being said. The church leaders looked back at him. They were calm. Direct. The room felt heavy.

Rick stood and held out his hand, dismissing Mitch. "We've checked the legalities with Willie, and you can give your resignation verbally. You don't need to write it down. For your own future ministry, you don't want a permanent record of this. Besides, this has dragged out long enough and done enough damage. . . . We'd like the whole thing to just go away. It's best for all concerned."

"You mean I don't have a say in this? You're just firing me? That's it?" Mitch said stunned, not offering Rick his hand back.

"We're not firing you, Mitch. Didn't you hear me? We're offering you a chance to resign, to leave with dignity. You know this is the best thing for everyone. No need to make it ugly. We'll give you four week's pay right now if you just walk out of this office, gather your things and go home. You are not to step foot in the youth ministry room again and you are not to talk to the students any more. No more contact with anyone from this church. Understood? This is the best offer you're going to get, Mitch. I'd take it if I were you."

Mitch felt arrested. He was at the mercy of the elders, and they were taking full advantage of his weakness. What other choice did he have than to take their offer? It was hard enough to find a youth ministry position to support a family. But if he was fired, no one would want to hire him. Besides, that four week's pay would be all the income they'd have. Mitch stood up, dejected, "Fine, I'll be out of here by the end of the day." And he walked out the door.

At the end of the hall, where Mitch's office was, were stacked boxes. They were full of his things. Someone, probably the janitor or church secretary, packed up his things while he was in Rick's office.

⁘

MY PARENTS CALL this duo-dating. I know it's stupid, but at least I get to go on dates," Steph said sheepishly, handing Jared the bread-basket. "Sorry, my parents insisted on coming."

"That's okay. At least they're sitting at another table. They aren't too bad, I guess. Nicer than my parents."

"Yeah, unless you have to live with them."

As the food arrived, Stephanie's parents came over. It was time for the Patterson family ritual. They did this at each meal.

"Aw, Dad, not tonight!" Steph quickly glanced over at Jared, obviously embarrassed.

"This is who we are, sweetie. Come on, stand up."

Jared stood next to Mr. Patterson as the entire family encircled the table. He grabbed Jared's hand, and led the blessing for the food. Everyone prayed, except Jared. Head bowed, eyes opened looking around the circle, this was his first experience with a Wiccan prayer.

"We are thankful for the bounty. We are thankful for the sacrifice. We are thankful for the blessing. Great mother, your blessings are numerous. Your care is unending. Strengthen us through this feast. Blessed be."

"Blessed be," Mr. Patterson said again, ending the prayer. Jared and Steph quickly sat back down, but Mr. Patterson had some unfinished business there.

"Say, Jared. What are you up to tomorrow?"

"Actually, I was going to help my dad change the oil in the car. That won't take all day, though. What do you have in mind?"

"Well, I've got some weeds that are killing plants in my flowerbed."

"I can help you with that," Jared volunteered, trying to make a good impression.

"Great. I'll be happy to pay you. And can you bring Paul? It's a pretty big job," Mr. Patterson smiled.

"No problem. We'll be over about nine."

As Mr. Patterson headed back to his seat, Jared looked over at Steph. She was beautiful! He couldn't believe that he actually scored a date with Stephanie Patterson. He couldn't stop staring at her.

Stephanie paused from eating her gourmet veggie-burger long enough to stare back at Jared. "Stop staring at me. You're creeping me out!"

"Sorry," Jared said averting his eyes. Looking back at her timidly, he asked, "If I asked you out again, would you go? This time without your parents?"

"I don't know," Stephanie looked boldly at Jared with a mysterious smile on her face. "I don't usually go out with the same guy twice."

Suddenly feeling gutsy, Jared said, "Well, I'm asking and I'll probably keep asking."

"Go ahead," she dared. "You never know!"

DEWITCHING WITCHCRAFT

We often forget that there is an ongoing struggle in Scripture between those who followed God, and the followers of other religions. We often glamorize the stories of our favorite biblical characters and imagine that they never struggled with duotheism or polytheism. We ignore their doubts about their monotheistic beliefs or their doubts in the divinity of Jesus. We gloss over the monotheistic struggle that runs throughout Scripture.

Truth is, throughout history, the belief in one God or the belief in God as described in Scripture are unique concepts. They were unique in ancient Mesopotamia during the dawn of humanity until the time of Jesus. They were unique in the New Testament times and throughout the history of the Church. So, these descriptions of witchcraft and how followers of God struggled against it are just glimpses of the ongoing struggle that existed throughout biblical times. It was not exclusive only to witchcraft: however, for our study, we'll limit ourselves only within the context of witchcraft and Satanism.

## The History of Witchcraft in the Bible

Almost from the beginning of their history, Israelites used magical practices to manipulate the outcome of a person's situation. Jacob practiced a crude form of animal husbandry by using a striped stick in the watering hole of his father-in-law's animals to make them weak.

This was an attempt to manipulate nature in order to produce a certain outcome. Ultimately Jacob got what he wanted, but God let him know that it was God who achieved the outcome, not Jacob's practices (Genesis 30:37–31:13).

Magic was practiced in Egypt in the book of Exodus. When Moses went before Pharaoh demanding the release of the Israelites, he followed God's directions and plagues were sent upon Egypt. Pharaoh's magicians were able to duplicate only some of the plagues, but weren't able to take any of the plagues away. Once again, God proved himself to be greater than the Egyptian magicians (Exodus 7:8–11:10).

*According to Wiccan sources, church officials used Leviticus 20:27 to support their witch persecution of the late 1600s. Throughout history religious and political leaders often quote from this verse to justify their searching out and killing of supposed witches.*

*Many scholars believe that the Golden Calf was a representation of the Apis god of Egyptian religion. The Apis was believed to represent power, and possibly the physical manifestation of the Pharaoh. The Apis god was the child of Osiris, making it a sibling god of Set. The worst sin you could commit against the Apis was to destruct its physical manifestation—the cow statue. So, when Moses destroyed the Golden Calf in Exodus, he committed a "sin" against the Egyptian religion, and in the eyes of the Israelites who trusted the Golden Calf.[1]*

Saul, the first king of Israel, drove out the mediums and the spiritists and forbade anyone to consult them. However, after Samuel died, Saul got scared and secretly visited a medium. Actually, Saul consulted the "witch of Endor" because God wouldn't answer him through the

Urim. The day after Saul consulted the witch, he died (1 Sam. 28, 31:1–6)

> *The woman described as a witch in the 1 Samuel passage was proficient in necromancy—contacting the spirits of dead people in the search for answers and advice. Common methods of necromancy today include the tarot, Ouija boards, and mediums.*

A few years later (after King David), Solomon, who was considered the "wise" king, allowed his many wives to bring their gods and religious practices to Jerusalem. This began an ugly cycle among the kings of Israel. One king would "do right in the eyes of the Lord" and the next would "do evil in the eyes of the Lord." The "evil" was the religious practices, which involved witchcraft that the kings chose (1 Sam.–2 Chron.).

> *The name Jezebel means "Where is the Prince?" which was a common cry of the followers of Baal when they believed Baal had gone into the Underworld.[2]*

As a result of Israel's spiritual faithlessness, God allowed their enemies to topple the important Israelite cities and take the Israelites into captivity. Several nations held them in captivity off and on until we find them under the rule of the Romans in the New Testament. While they were in captivity (or on the run either hiding from their captors, or trying to find a new home) the Israelites took many opportunities to participate in the worship of other gods and adopt witchcraft.

Witchcraft was alive and well in New Testament culture. In fact, Acts tells us about three specific people who practiced witchcraft. The first was a Samaritan named Simon (Acts 8:9–25). The second was a

Jewish sorcerer named Bar-Jesus (aka, Elymas) (Acts 13:4–12). The third was a group of people in Ephesus, both Jews and Greeks, who practiced sorcery. When this group chose to believe in the name of Jesus and the message of the gospel of Christ that Paul brought them, they burned their sorcery scrolls publicly.

From the time that Satan deceived Adam and Eve in the Garden of Eden until the time of the early church in the New Testament, we see witchcraft peppered throughout the Bible. And in many instances, it was enticing enough to lure God's people into its practice.

## THE TAROT VS. THE URIM AND THUMIM

The tarot is a deck of cards used to contact spirits (or have spirits contact us) for the purpose of telling the future. These cards are used by a variety of faiths, including Wiccans. Satanists don't seem to have much patience with the tarot, probably because it's too tame and laid back for their antagonistic worldview. In addition to the tarot, humans have tried to read the stars (astrology), contact the dead through séances (necromancy), and make other attempts at predicting the future.

The Bible has its own kind of divination device in the Urim and Thumim. Scholars disagree about what this device was. The general consensus is that they were probably two flat stones with yes and no printed on either side, or of a certain color on either side. They were usually only used by the priestly class in order to discern the will of God for a particular situation. In cases when the Israelites desired to know God's will, they would go to the priest who would use this tool to divine God's will or opinion on their matter.

The differences between this tool and the divination tactics in witchcraft are obvious. Where ancient witchcraft relied on signs (astrology), or dead spirits (necromancy, mediums) to figure out the future, the Israelites relied on their ongoing relationship with God and one ordained method for figuring out his desires in his peoples lives. In Scripture, we see that the use of witchcraft builds a reliance on self for the understanding of one's future. The priests used the Urim and Thumim as God directed (Exodus 28:30), thus, they built reliance on God rather than on themselves.

## FORTUNE TELLERS VS. PROPHETS OF THE LORD

Fortune tellers have predicted the future through several means. Some have read palms, while others have used tarot cards or contacted the dead. As we learned throughout the book, each culture has had its own method of telling the future. Even the Israelites had the Urim and Thumim. How do these compare to the prophets of the Old Testament? Are their practices similar? With so much attention in the Bible focused on revealing the future, how is this different from fortune telling?

Prophecies fill a good portion of the Bible. In fact, the last seventeen books of the Old Testament are prophetic books. Later, in the Gospels, Jesus prophesied about the End Days. And there are prophetic letters late in the New Testament that predict specific end times events.

To understand the difference between fortune telling and prophesying, you need to think globally for a moment. The prophecies in the Old and New Testaments are general in nature, and yet specific enough to offer hints about what was coming. They were specific enough to tell the Jews what to look for in the coming Messiah. When they deal with specific truths about the world, they don't predict days or hours, they paint general pictures. When they speak to specific events in the lives of individuals, they paint general, not specific pictures. Globally speaking, the prophecies in the Bible read more like, "Folks, this major event will happen. It is imminent. Get ready." Whereas, in fortune telling and other divination attempts, the idea is to reach into the world of the dead or spirit realm for specific answers.

In revealing prophecy, God had a relationship with the people he was prophesying to. His prophecies were and are relationally based. They're to warn people he loves. They're not an attempt to reveal for revelation's sake. Rather, the prophecies in Scripture usually present the recipients with a choice to follow God and listen to him. They're a calling back to God, not a promise of endless happiness and wealth. Additionally, prophets cannot break into the divine realm and *force* an answer from God's hand (as often appears in common divination practices). Prophecy is a revelation from God, not a pursuit by man.

## MAGIC VS. MIRACLES

We've learned a lot about magic in this book. We've seen that magic is the attempt by humans to manipulate the spiritual world in ways that achieve results in the physical world. Magic is a personal pursuit for personal gain. Rarely do witches perform magic for others. A distinction has arisen about magic—it falls into two different categories. One category includes magic that is accomplished through the manipulation of natural forces. Another kind of magic is used to reach into the spiritual realm to accomplish results in the physical world.

To some people, Jesus' miracles in the New Testament appear as a kind of otherworldly magic, as though Jesus the magician wandered Galilee and Judah manipulating the physical world for the benefit of others. The fact that he constantly addressed the spirit world (in the form of casting out demons) must have associated tales about his miracles with stories about how he connected the spiritual and physical worlds for the healing of mankind. In fact, Scripture notes that as Jesus was healing people, onlookers and church leaders actually did question his source of power to do miracles (Matthew 12:22–28). This demonstrates that then, as well as today, the miraculous is often mistaken for magic.

*Understanding the difference between a* miracle *and* magic *is easy.* Magic *is the attempt to manipulate the spiritual to act for selfish means. A* miracle *is the Divine breaking into our time and physical space to change a present reality for our benefit.*

A miracle isn't magic, although without the understanding of the source or purpose of the event, it does appear as a magical event. A miracle is God breaking into his created universe and order to change the physical, spiritual, and emotional lives of humans by doing something that no other being can accomplish. The Red Sea, manna in the desert, healing blind people, casting out demons—those were events that only God, Jesus, or his power in the disciples could do. Only he and his power could accomplish them because only he created the universe. As creator, only God can manipulate the creation. God is the only being that stands outside the universe and has the power to break into it.

*For some, the power of Jesus' miracles closely aligns him as being a Wiccan. After all, he was able to manipulate physical elements like air and water. However, Jesus demonstrated that he was in no way connected with any form of witchcraft. He related all power to his Heavenly Father (God) as the source for his power. He communicated with God through prayer, demonstrating a relationship with him. There was no impersonal force, and no ceremonial attempts to manipulate nature. As God, Jesus had, and continues to have, power over his creation.*

Magic, the humanly created method of connecting with the spirit world for selfish benefit is a reverse and skewed attempt that demonstrates spiritual hunger. While magic demonstrates humanity's hunger for a touch of the divine, it reverses the order of how the divine reaches humanity. It's interesting that humans strive to ignore the hand of the creator in the universe, yet attempt to accomplish divine results in the physical world. Humanity is passionate about denying God's power, and yet they're hungry to see the effects of his power.

## THE POLITICALLY INCORRECT GOD

You've got to ask yourself, what's the big deal? Why is the God of the Bible so intolerant toward the practice of witchcraft? Why can't we choose to practice religion in any way we see fit? After all, don't we have free will? Don't we have the ability to think on our own? Do we have to be puppets of this biblical God?

> *The Bible is religiously intolerant. In many cases major biblical figures didn't tolerate the teaching or belief of people of other faiths. These biblical characters stood strong, even when they faced persecution for their "intolerance."*

Throughout Scripture, God warns his people not to be duped by frauds who claim to be god. He proves over and over again throughout Scripture, using miracles and signs, that he is the one who created everything in the universe. He sent prophets to testify that he is the one true God. Still, people chose to believe in the fraud rather than the Truth.

## BATTLE OF TWO FAITHS

Jesus, the instigator who began the new religious movement in the world and who was the perfect, sinless God-man, faced the source of Wicca and Satanism. In Matthew 4:1–11 Satan tempted Jesus in three specific ways. First, Jesus was tempted to use his power to feed himself. Second, Jesus was tempted to test God's powers of protection. Third, Jesus was tempted with the opportunity to have possession of the entire world. As a response to all of these, Jesus relied on Scripture as the chief method of rebuffing Satan's tests.

Other than to prepare Jesus for his ministry, why was Jesus tempted by Satan like this? Scholars and thinkers better than I have written long texts about the temptations of Jesus. They've theorized and calculated about the reasons for this event. There has been and always will be the wrestling between witchcraft and Satanism. Satan will continue to tempt with alternative beliefs, with the hope that he can persuade us to use powers we don't understand to achieve results we don't need and can't handle.

It's no wonder that witchcraft is interesting, exciting, powerful, and tempting to so many. It makes sense that humans would be intrigued by the opportunity to control the elements of the universe. It's easy to understand that the chance to summon darker spirits would thrill some people. Certainly, the chance to use magic to get rid of enemies, gain more money, get a better job, fall in love with the "perfect" person all seem to be positive aspects of witchcraft. It makes sense that the best word to use here is in fact the word we've used throughout this chapter. It has been a *struggle* throughout history between witchcraft and Christianity. As long as the Lord delays in returning with the New Heaven and Earth, the *struggle* will continue.

Aren't these the same kind of temptations Jesus faced? In our waiting for God, Satan tempts us with things we want, offers a spectacular means for obtaining them, and giggles when we succumb. Like Jesus, we face the daily opportunity to choose the easier road.

Our obligation as believers is to surrender ourselves to God, who takes control and guides us into everything—possessions, occupations, love, etc. God often leads us into things we could only dream of by taking us down roads we either don't expect or get tired of walking. God's plans for us are bigger and grander than our minds could even dream. The person who trusts God finds their security in his love for them. It is a humbling, exciting, and awe-inspiring experience to see God, who loves you, working on your behalf.

# Chapter 14

# THE TO DO LIST
*Myths About Wicca*

*I*'m glad you all could come out for this meeting. Please forgive the lateness of the hour. We've had a sad development in the youth ministry and need you to know what our next steps are."

Behind Rick sat the elders of C4. Their faces expressed sympathy for the parents.

Rick continued, "Mitch McCorkle, our youth pastor over the last several years, has decided to quit. We're not sure what's going on with him. He stormed into a meeting I was having with the elders yesterday. I believe his exact words were, 'I'll be out of here by the end of the day.' Then he left. He didn't even bother giving a written resignation. So we don't even know why he's doing this. We tried speaking with him, but he didn't want to hear anything we had to say. By the time the elders' meeting ended, Mitch had cleaned out his office and was gone. He won't be coming back."

Marcie Collins stood up. "I tried calling Mitch a few hours go. He answered the phone, but when he found out it was me, he said that he couldn't talk to me and he hung up."

"Yes, I was afraid that Mitch would do this. I suspect that he's struggling with a deep spiritual issue. You see, when you're out of whack spiritually, you can quickly become unstable. I'm thinking he's been unstable for quite some time now. I invited him to come tonight to speak with you himself, but he refused. He's refusing to talk to all of us. My advice is not to contact him. Just give him some space. All we can do at this point is to pray for him."

Rick's oily words took on an authoritative tone. Heads nodded around the room. Concern for Mitch and his family spread across the faces of parents.

"However, I want to reassure you that the youth ministry at C4 will remain as strong as ever. While we search for a new youth pastor, I've asked my oldest son, Pete, to take over. He's worked with youth before in a volunteer role. Mitch left with a full calendar of events, so it won't be hard to pick up where he left off. I'm sure Pete will want to tweak it some to add his own personality and passion to the ministry. Of course, I will be working alongside him helping out in any way I can; although I doubt he'll need it." Rick smiled and motioned for Pete to join him at the front of the room.

Pete stood up and made a short speech outlining his vision for the youth ministry while the search for a new youth pastor began.

⁂

JACK PATTERSON WAS standing in his driveway when Jared and Paul pulled up.

"Hey, great, you're here! Let's get to work." He said, leading Paul and Jared to the back yard."

"See here, Jared, this is what I was telling you about. The weeds are all over. They've grown into the hydrangeas. They've already killed the other plants. Let's see what we can do to get rid of this."

Jack, Jared, and Paul pulled for hours before Jared stood up, and stretched his back. "Mr. Patterson?"

"Jack, please. Just call me Jack."

"Alright, uh, Jack, This would go a lot quicker if we had some clippers. Do you have any?"

"Great idea, Jared. I knew I made the right decision to hire you. The clippers are hanging in the garage next to the shelf with the paint. Go ahead and get them."

Jared headed in the direction of the garage. The garage's neat organization should have made finding the clippers easy. Unfortunately, Jared couldn't find them. He looked everywhere, but no dice.

"Jack!" Jared called from the garage. "I don't see the clippers!"

"They're in there somewhere, Jared. If they're not on the wall, just look around."

Jared kept looking. He flipped through a pile of newspapers stacked neatly in the corner. He felt around on top of large, plastic storage containers marked "Samhain." He looked around the garage trying to find the most logical place for the clippers. Toward the back of the garage, Jared saw a door.

*I've looked everywhere else,* Jared thought to himself. *That must be where he keeps them.*

The door was creaky and dirty. Jared poked his head into the room and looked around. "No tools here. But something in the corner caught his eye. He had to check it out.

He walked slowly past the pictures on the wall toward the corner where a table sat. The musty smell of the room combined with the scent of candles. A small notebook, candles, symbols, ancient looking things and brand new things were placed precisely around the table. Jared studied them. It looked similar to the table at the house on Denver Street. The dark room offered just enough light for Jared to look through the small notebook sitting on the table. The book was entitled "Patterson."

Jared couldn't help but pick it up. Out of the middle of the journal fell a loose page with a long to do list printed in neat handwriting. The items at the end of the list jumped out at Jared.

47. Mary—Stephanie (crossed out)

48. See if Rick can help with Mitch. (crossed out)

49. Meet with Chief Collins (crossed out)

50. Get to know the boys—Jack

51. Hook up with Mitch—Janet

52. Shelby—Stephanie

*So . . . what am I looking at here,* Jared thought to himself. Further up the list, his name had been crossed through a few times. Obviously there was history here. This took effort, scheming. There was a plan of some sort and Jared was involved as an object of it.

Jared noticed the pictures on the wall, the ones he walked past when he entered the small room. There were pictures of Mary, Shelby, Jared, and Paul. Also, there were pictures of kids he'd never talked to but had seen at school. Next to those were pictures of Mary's mom and dad. Next to each picture was at least one name from the Patterson family. Next to Jared's name: Jack Patterson. Next to Shelby and Mary's name: Steph. Stephanie's mom's name was next to Mary's parents. The arrangement of the pictures reminded Jared of the kind of strategy he learned during his only year on the football team in junior high. It was sort of an offense-defense arrangement.

The scene was overwhelming. Jared looked around the room and slowly began backing out. *Should he take the pictures? Steal the journal? Tell someone? But who?* Jared backed into Janet Patterson standing in the doorway.

"How did you get in here?" Janet accused. Jared's heart skipped a few beats. His fingertips tingled with heat. His breathing became shallow.

Barely able to speak above a whisper, he answered, "Jack said the clippers were in the garage. I couldn't find them, so I thought they might be in here."

"This room is supposed to be locked. You're not supposed to be in here."

"I . . . I'm not sure. I don't know. The clippers. Jack sent me in for the clippers. I have to go."

Jared squeezed past Janet and headed for the backyard. "Paul, we've gotta go. Now!" Jared ordered.

"Dude, I'm not done here," Paul argued.

"I don't care! Come on." Paul could hear the urgency in Jared's voice. Without any more argument, Paul got up and the boys headed for the car.

As the boys roared down the street, Janet walked into the backyard and stood next to Jack. "Jared found the altar. What should we do?"

"I thought I locked that room. Well, it's not a problem I guess. It'll all get worked out soon enough. Let's move the stuff out of the room, just in case Jared talks to someone."

## DEWITCHING WITCHCRAFT

Probably the most frustrating aspect of Wicca and Satanism is that they're difficult to define. Their beliefs often stretch beyond the mysterious and are impossible to unravel. Their histories are always debated. Their true meanings are often hidden. And, because many Wiccans and Satanists have felt they've been at the center of much religious persecution, it can be difficult to find one who will openly discuss their beliefs. Even if you were able to persuade a Wiccan or

Satanist to discuss their beliefs, you're likely to only get *their* opinion or understanding. Wicca and Satanism's structure is highly personalized, making the religion different with each person.

All of this makes these two religions nearly impossible to completely understand. Because they defy understanding, many sincere (and some not so sincere) people have made claims about Wicca and Satanism that are untrue. As people have vocalized their claims, many of the untrue ones have slowly become fact. Consequently, much misinformation about Wicca and Satanism has spread, making it even more difficult to understand their true natures.

Following are a *few* of the most popular myths, with a little explanation and analysis after each one.

## HOLLYWOOD IS RUN BY WICCANS AND SATANISTS

This is a claim made by many Christians seeking to find a source for the openly evil movies and television shows prevalent in modern culture. This is an extremely difficult myth to prove or disprove. In recent years, a number of Christians have "come out of the closet" in Hollywood, speaking openly about their belief in God and their acceptance of Christian teachings. Obviously (based on the movies that are released), there is strong support for Wiccan teachings, and many movies have been released that promote or teach Wiccan beliefs. However, the industry that makes movies is, most probably, very religiously diverse, including people who believe in Pagan, satanic, New Age, Mormon, and occult beliefs, among others.

One minor exception to this might be in the television industry. I say this because the television shows that promote Wiccan beliefs clearly outnumber those of other religions. At the writing of this book, television shows like *Charmed, Buffy the Vampire Slayer, Sabrina the Teenage Witch* are in regular rotation. While these shows don't teach an accurate concept of Wicca or Satanism, they are openly devoted to teaching many of the beliefs found in both religions.

## HARRY POTTER PROMOTES WITCHCRAFT

The most common modern reference to witchcraft is usually joined with a mention of the Harry Potter book series by J.K. Rowling, and the subsequent movies. There are already a number of books written about the connection (or lack thereof) between the books and witchcraft.

Here are a few items that are worth noting:

### DIFFERENCES BETWEEN HARRY POTTER AND WITCHCRAFT

- *Magic.* The magic used in Harry Potter is a cartoonish form where the believer says magical words and something happens in the physical world. Wiccan magic is much different, requiring much time in preparing spells, and much time in actually casting the spell (including raising power and performing a ritual).

- *Flying.* Witches do not fly in the physical world. However, in the Harry Potter stories, the young witches fly on several occasions.

- *Talking hats, animation of inanimate objects, giants and strange beings.* Harry Potter stories include the fantastic element, which makes the story interesting. There are giant dogs and people. Objects seem to have human personalities, wills, powers and abilities. These are the stuff of story, and not a part of modern witchcraft.

### SIMILARITIES BETWEEN HARRY POTTER AND WITCHCRAFT

- Both Harry Potter and witchcraft believe that reality can be changed or enhanced through spells and ritual. This connects them together in worldview.

- Both believe that there is regular interaction between the physical world and the spirit world. This is obvious in Wicca, as we have seen earlier in this book. In Harry Potter, this is seen through the appearance of ghosts, and spirits who come in and out of the story.

- Both believe in dimensions of existence beyond the physical world. Wicca has its varying degrees of existence. The Harry Potter story clearly demonstrates that humans can interact and travel to different planes of existence.

The one similarity between witchcraft and Harry Potter is in theme. Harry Potter promotes witchcraft as fun, easy, acceptable, and appropriate. This makes Harry Potter somewhat of a gateway belief, making Wicca easier to accept. Obviously, the beliefs found in Harry Potter go directly against Christianity.

## Many Popular Musicians Are Involved in Witchcraft

When I was sixteen, this statement was perpetuated by the idea of backward masking. Good Christian leaders would corral students in a room, teach them about all the evils of secular music. Then, students would listen to records backward and hear crazy statements supposedly interlaced with the music. The thinking was that these statements worked their way through your ears, into your minds, and corrupted your souls. Is this possible? Is the music industry out to convert students to Wicca and Satanism? Are there satanic or Wiccan musicians?

The truth is, it depends on your thinking. Music is not inherently evil or good. Music is a tool that can be used for either. And, obviously, music in the hands of a Satanist or Wiccan will be used to promote their beliefs, just like music in the hands of a Christian can be used in the same manner. Executives and musicians in the music industry come from a variety of religious traditions. Certainly, some of these people are possibly from Wiccan or satanic traditions. Some are possibly from Christian traditions as well. Three things should be noted in this discussion.

First, all people, including Christians should carefully screen all music they purchase or listen to. Since not every song is glorifying to God or edifying for the believer, Christians must be careful about the music they listen to and carefully scrutinize it according to their own standards.

Second, not every non-Christian band is evil or good. Again, we must be careful. Just because a musician wears a pentagram, it doesn't mean they actually are Satanists. Because a singer sings about loving God, that does not make them a Christian. Believers must be cautious, and think about the music they listen to.

Third, the modern (humanistic) definition of satanic and the biblical definition of satanic are both extremely important to the Christian in regards to music. Obviously, every song that praises Satan or another god as being powerful or supreme should be avoided. However, songs that promote following human desires or worshiping humanity should also be avoided. These songs support the modern, more atheistic view of Satan, and are just as dangerous.

## WITCHES RIDE BROOMS AND FLOAT

Witches don't ride brooms or float. This myth is the result of misinformed people from the Middle Ages, who attempted to create wild, untrue tales about witches. Today, some witches do use brooms during rituals to symbolically sweep away negative energy. However, they don't ride them.

## WITCHES WEAR BLACK CAPES AND TALL, POINTED HATS

This myth seems to have developed in the medieval times. Witches were known to wear cloaks for a variety of reasons. There is no standard uniform for witches today. However, most witches wear pentagrams and Satanists wear baphomets as symbols of power. One of the most popular "celebrity" witches today is Fiona Horne, who appeared in a 2004 television series *Mad Mad House*. On that show, Horne changed the traditional concept of a witch by wearing modern clothes and appearing very contemporary. Horne demonstrates that the old concept of Wicca as ugly and scary is a thing of the past.

## WITCHES HIDE IN THE WOODS

This was probably a claim invented by people who knew that witches worshiped in nature (in the woods) and feared going into the woods for fear of running into witches. It's true that many witches worship in the woods, claiming that worshiping and spellcasting in the woods creates a closer connection to the energy and power of the universe. But they don't hide there or wait there to kidnap people.

## WICCANS AND SATANISTS TORTURE, ABUSE, AND KILL CHILDREN

The history on this myth is sketchy. Some people have claimed that Wiccans and Satanists have kidnapped and abused helpless children for centuries. Some of these tales probably surfaced during the infamous witch trials in the Middle Ages. In recent history, some people have claimed that Satanists have taken them or their children and sexually abused them, or murdered them. This has become known as satanic ritual abuse. In the mid-1980s, there was a flurry of media attention on this subject. Claims were accompanied by evidence of abuse, but were also rebutted by Satanists, who maintained they did not participate in abuse. Today, people are still debating whether Satanists physically abuse others. Since Satanists and Wiccans deny their religious practices include harming people, either Satanists are lying, those claiming the abuse are lying or ritual abuse is practiced by splinter groups loosely associated with these religions.

## WICCANS AND SATANISTS KILL ANIMALS

Much like the previous claim, some have witnessed or discovered the remains of an animal, which has been killed or gutted, surrounded by satanic or demonic symbols. Numerous television shows document the findings of pentagrams in remote places with the remains of animals, apparently sacrificed in a ritualistic fashion. It's difficult to completely know what religion actually practices the ritualistic killing of animals. As with the abuse of children discussed above, Satanists and Wiccans deny any involvement. However, in some religions associated with Satanism, the killing of animals is associated with ritual, spellcasting, and power.

## WITCHES CAST SPELLS ON PEOPLE

This is a myth, and both Christians and Wiccans have contributed to it. Here are some of the different slants both parties have put on this "myth."

### THE CHRISTIAN MYTH OF SPELL CASTING:

Possibly out of fear, or out of misunderstanding, many people have claimed that witches cast spells on people to harm them. Witches claim this is not true. Witches do cast spells, but not all of their spells are to hurt or kill people. Witches claim that Christianity's fear and hatred of other religions has led to lies about spell casting.

### THE WICCAN MYTH OF SPELL CASTING:

Wiccans often promote that they are kind, gentle and easygoing people, especially when they use spells and incantations. They promote their spells as mostly benign, aimed at helping the spellcaster. While this is mostly true, it is not completely true. In fact, if you search the Internet, you'll find stories about witches who claim to have cast spells to harm people. There is even a class of witches who are known to cast spells on others called "Black Witches."

THE TRUTH ABOUT SPELL CASTING:

On at least two occasions, as I've been researching this project, I've run into two different Wiccans (not connected to each other in any way) who have claimed to have harmed someone through casting a spell. Obviously, these stories are just claims by people and can't be corroborated. The truth about casting spells to harm people probably varies from witch to witch, since each one has their own personal moral code they obey.

## WITCHES ARE EVIL, AND ALWAYS SEEK TO DO HARM

This myth has a myriad of sources, and many people are to blame for it. The most culpable party are Wiccans, because of the secrecy of their craft.

There are two categories of witches within Wicca. We learned about these categories when we discussed magic. "White" witches are said to be more morally concerned and unwilling to harm other people. "Black" witches don't care about harming other people and disregard the Rule of Three. These witches are said to cast spells aimed at harming people. Some witches aim to do harm, and the larger population of witches, who claim that they're peaceful, loving people, don't always embrace them.

## SATANISTS WORSHIP THE DEVIL

If, by now, you've missed this point in the book, I put it here as a reminder. Not all Satanists worship the devil. Many, in fact, are atheists and are attracted to Satanism because of its heightened view of humanity. Others worship the *idea* of Satan because they reject Christianity, and worshiping "Satan" represents their disdain for traditional Christian beliefs. However, it's very true that many people worship an actual Satan, who they believe really exists and has very real power in the physical world.

Ultimately, from a Christian perspective, everyone who doesn't worship Jesus Christ, worships Satan.

## WITCHES WORSHIP SATAN

Again, if you missed this in the book, this one is restated here to remind you. Witches in the Wiccan tradition claim to have no connection to Satan. They claim not to worship Satan. They claim not to even believe that Satan exists. Again, Christians believe that anyone who doesn't worship God worships Satan.

## SATANISTS CAN CAST DEMONS INTO YOU

Some believe that Satanists who believe in Satan as an actual being can cast demons into people. They believe that demons can harm people in the physical world, that they can be oppressed or possessed by the demonic. Is any of this really true?

### CAN HUMANS BE POSSESSED BY DEMONS?

Yes. These days, you don't need to search very far to find stories of people who claim to have been possessed by demons. And, there are many modern-day exorcists who tell of instances where they've cast demons out of people (and some even televise these events). Scripture gives many clear examples of people who were possessed by demons, as in Luke 4:31–37 where Jesus drives out demons from a man who is verbally attacking Jesus. Jesus casts the demons out of the man, demonstrating that humans can be possessed. This story also demonstrates that the only hope people who are possessed have in being delivered is through Jesus Christ.

CAN CHRISTIANS BE POSSESSED BY DEMONS?

It's logical to ask that if *humans* can be possessed by a demon, can *Christians*? Since the Spirit of the Living God inhabits believers, is demon possession possible? Modern theological thought relies more on human thinking here, than on Scripture. There is no solid irrefutable Scripture that can be quoted that conclusively states that Christians can't be possessed. We can't even infer this idea from any of the miracles Jesus or an apostle performed, since we're not given much background on the people who received miracles in Scripture. However, what many organizations teach on this topic seems logical. Since the Spirit of God inhabits a believer, it would be impossible for God's spirit and a demon to exist in the same being. Therefore, it seems completely impossible that a Christian can be possessed by a demon.

People who claim to be both fully devoted to God, and also possessed by a demon should examine both their conversion, and their interpretation of the demonic activity in their lives.

CAN DEMONS HARM YOU?

Maybe the question is better stated, "Can the evil spiritual world mentally, physically or spiritually oppress you?" The early church believed that even though someone believed in Christ, they could still be affected by the evil spiritual world without actually being possessed (Ephesians 6:10–13). This is further demonstrated by the temptation of Jesus in the wilderness (Matthew 4:1-11). Believers and non-believers who are oppressed and influenced by the demonic world should rely on the biblical principles in Ephesians 6 as a starting point for resisting satanic influences in their lives.

# Chapter 15

# THE TRUTH COMES OUT

*Tying Up Loose Ends*

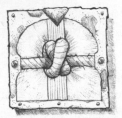

*S*o, are you going to tell me what's going on?" Paul came to a stop at the red light.

"Dude, there was a room in the garage with pictures of us, the McCorkles, Shelby, and some others. There was this table with some sort of voodoo stuff all over it. They had our pictures on the wall!" Jared's voice cracked.

"Whoa! Slow down! I'm not following." Paul said.

"You haven't seen Mary all week, have you? And Mitch wasn't at RealWalk. No one knew where he was." Jared was panicked.

"What are you saying?" Paul was getting nervous.

"It started with cows. Maybe they've upgraded to humans. I think we should go to Chief Collins and tell him what I found."

"No! Before we go to him, we need to check things out on our own. Let's go to the McCorkles and see what we can find."

❧

THE PHONE RANG in Rick's office. He and Pete were in the middle of re-working the youth ministry at C4. All traces of Mitch's influence needed to be removed.

"Hello, this is Pastor Rick."

"Rick, this is Janet," the voice on the other end said.

"What's up?"

"Jack had the bright idea to send Jared into the garage to find the clippers."

"Yeah, so?" Rick was annoyed.

"He found our altar. The pictures were on the wall and the list was on the table. I'm afraid of who he might tell."

"Don't worry about him. Gather everyone together tonight at Potts. Once we finish, no one will believe a word he says," Rick assured her.

Rick swiveled back around and hung up the phone. Leaning back in his chair, he drummed his fingers on his mouth, deep in thought.

"What's wrong, Dad? Who was that?" Pete asked.

"Oh, uh, we have some unfinished business tonight at Potts. Get your Denver Street group together. Have Steph get everything from the Denver Street house. This could get messy."

⁂

PAUL SLOWLY EASED the car to a stop along the curb in front of the McCorkles house. He and Jared sat for a minute and just looked at the house. Nothing seemed out of place. The McCorkles car was parked in the driveway, the empty trash can still sat on the sidewalk. Everything seemed quiet . . . almost too quiet.

"Well, let's get this over with," Paul said, shaking himself back to reality.

"Okay," Jared's voice cracked. "I'm right behind you."

They got out of the car and crept quietly up the walk. Peeking in the windows, they noticed boxes and newspapers strewn all over the room. Something was wrong.

"Listen," Paul said, "we'll knock on the door first, but if no one answers, we'll have to break it down."

Paul knocked on the door. No answer. He knocked again, this

time a little louder.

"Just a minute!" they heard a voice inside.

The door opened and there stood Sandy looking at them questioningly. "What do you want boys?"

"We need to talk to Mitch. Is he here?" Paul asked.

"Yes, but he can't speak with you. You boys will have to leave." She said, blocking the door.

"No. We have to see him now!" Jared said, pushing past her.

Paul looked at her sheepishly, shrugged, and the two of them followed Jared into the house.

Jared burst into Mitch's office. "Mitch, we have to talk."

❧

"SHELBY?"

"No, this is her mom. Can I help you?"

"Oh, hi Mrs. Collins. This is Stephanie Patterson. I was wondering if I might speak with Shelby?"

"Just a minute, Stephanie. I'll go and get her."

As Steph waited on hold, her adrenaline started pumping. This was going to be a night to remember. She was excited.

"Hey, Steph, what's up?"

"Hey, Shel. I've got your first assignment. Are you ready for it?"

"Sure, whatever you need."

"It's very simple. I need for you to get Paul, Jared, and the McCorkles to Potts tonight."

"No problem. See ya there."

"Bye," Steph hung up the phone and smiled.

❧

MITCH LOOKED UP from the box he was packing. "I'm sorry, Jared, but I can't speak with you. You'll have to leave now."

"What's going on?" Jared suddenly noticed that Mitch was packing. "Where are you going?"

"We're moving," Mitch responded. "I was asked to resign this week. I've accepted another position in my home church. Now, if you'll excuse me, I have a lot of packing to do."

Jared sat down, stunned. "It's all beginning to make sense. I can't believe it." Jared began to mumble.

Mitch looked over at Paul for help. "Listen, Mitch, it's real important that you hear what we've found. Just hear us out. Ten minutes is all we ask."

Unsure, Mitch finally conceded, "Okay, guys, come on in to the living room."

Once they were seated, Jared began, "Well, I guess it all started the night we decided to go to the house on Denver Street. You know 1800?"

"He already knows all about it," Mary interrupted, coming around the corner. She slowly lifted her head and looked at the boys.

"Whoa, what happened to you?" Paul asked.

Mary's lip was beginning to heal, but she was still pretty bruised. "It's a long story. I'd rather not repeat it. Besides, it doesn't matter anymore, we're leaving town."

"Well, he doesn't know this," Jared continued. Without taking a breath, he spilled the whole story of the room in the garage.

## DEWITCHING WITCHCRAFT

Perhaps you've read this far and still have lingering questions. Maybe more application oriented. The most pressing question might be, "So what are we to do about all of this?" We know that Christianity is polarized against Wicca and Satanism. We know that these two beliefs aren't compatible in any way with Christianity. We know that the Bible specifically warns against combining our understanding of God with other beliefs, including Wicca and Satanism. What do we do with all of this information?

It seems logical that Paul would have some things to say to believers today about how to face opposing beliefs including extreme ones like Wicca and Satanism. So, if you'll permit me . . . here are a few of the truths from Paul's writings that I believe fit well with our study of Wicca and Satanism.

## BEING YOKED WITH UNBELIEF

The Church in Corinth knew the struggle that believers face when they're confronted with opposing beliefs. Corinth was an intellectual city close to Athens, the center of Greek thought.

Corinth was a hub of strange sexual practices. Pagan Corinthian cults had mixed religious beliefs with sexual practices to create temples to Apollo and Aphrodite, which employed over a thousand temple prostitutes. Some of the economy in Corinth relied on this prostitution. Corinthian women were so loose that they became renown for their promiscuity. In ancient times, to call a woman "Corinthian" was akin to calling her sexually loose.

As the church was birthed in Corinth (probably about 51 AD, see Acts 18:1–18), it faced an ongoing onslaught of sexual temptation, intellectual heresies, and idolatry. As a warning to keep away from the immoral practices, and an encouragement to stay on track with their commitment to Christ, Paul writes these words:

Do not be yoked together with unbelievers. For what do righteousness and wickedness have in common? Or, what fellowship can light have with darkness? What harmony is there between Christ and Belial? What does a believer have in common with an unbeliever? What agreement is there between the temple of God and idols? (2 Cor. 6:14–16)

Paul's words to the believers in Corinth provide an excellent framework for us to apply some basic principles on the struggles between Christianity and Wicca and Satanism.

## PAUL'S CAUTION TODAY

Why would Paul write these words to believers? Possibly because he knew that the believers in Corinth *were* yoking themselves with the false teachers. He knew that they were joining with temple prostitutes. He understood the level which they had combined their beliefs in Jesus with other cultic beliefs. Paul knew something about believers and false teachers—that the two can't coexist.

Obviously, no Christian would willingly associate themselves with satanic beliefs. However, because we live in a pluralistic society, religious beliefs of all faiths and understandings are sprinkled everywhere.

Paul's words about yoking apply here. Believers have to *live cautiously*, and not yoke themselves with subtle Wiccan influences. Believers must be *aware* of the variety of philosophies, religions, beliefs, and practices of the people around them, or in the influences they allow into their lives. People who claim that Jesus is Savior, and omnipotent king must *evaluate* the kinds of material they view or read. It doesn't do any good to begin listing the *kinds* of influences that are evil, or the ones that teach against Christianity. Believers must possess a keen eye, always looking for deceptive philosophies.

Obviously, the important thing to remember here is to ask ourselves a few questions as we're taking in any media, such as:

- What beliefs does this movie/song preach? How is this contrary to my personal beliefs?

- What is the writer's perspective? How does this compare with my Christian beliefs?

- Do I understand the truth of Christianity about the subject being portrayed?

- How does this message specifically contradict Scripture?

- To what extent am I able to get close to this belief without personally being affected by it?

These aren't exciting kind of questions, and honestly none of us will ask them all the time, and in each moment we're listening or watching or reading. I look at those questions as a kind of application to John's words in 1 John 4:1–6 where he instructs believers to "test the spirits." Although John is speaking more about testing false teachers, we can apply this truth to the testing of the kind of everyday spirits we confront.

## SPIRITUAL WARFARE

Acts 19:1–41 records Paul being chased around in Ephesus by a band of angry cult worshipping folks. According to the story, the group worshipped Artemis (also called Diana) and they also made a hefty profit from her worshippers. The group is upset that Paul's preaching will damage their economy.

This experience must have been in his mind when he later wrote the believers in Ephesus the following words:

Put on the full armor of God so that you can take your stand against the devil's schemes. For our struggle is not against flesh and blood, but against the rulers, against the authorities, against the powers of this dark world and against the spiritual forces of evil in the heavenly realms. Therefore put on the full armor of

God, so that when the day of evil comes, you may be able to stand your ground, and after you have done everything, to stand. (Eph. 6:10–13)

When we consider what we might have to say to Wiccans and Satanists, we have to take notes from Paul's life. Although Paul spent much time as a theologian debating truth (see Acts 17:16–31), he also spent a considerable amount of time communicating a clear and simple salvation message. Paul even notes this in his letter to the Corinthian believers when he says, "We preach Christ crucified" (1 Corinthians1:23). Over and over, this is the message that Paul preaches, and it's also the message that he defends.

Speaking the truth about Christ *"stirs up the forces of evil in the heavenly realms."* When believers tell the truth about Christ in their lives, they should be prepared for the battle that results in sharing this truth.

Paul's words to the believers in Ephesus demonstrate a few interesting points:

*Paul assumes spiritual warfare.* We don't get a full explanation about what exactly Paul understood about the spiritual realm. This is possibly because Paul meant to focus more on the active life of the believer rather than an ongoing spiritual war. However, Paul doesn't take time to explain why believers experience spiritual warfare. Paul assumes that believers understand it as an element of an active faith in Christ.

*Paul also assumes the protection of God.* He doesn't stop and say, "When we experience warfare, here are the twenty ways we know that God will protect us." Paul explains the tools of spiritual warfare from the perspective of the protection of God. The weapons are given by God, who wants his children protected.

As in Paul's day, we certainly face all kind of temptations. There is no shortage of opportunities to sin, and new and creative ways to sin always confront us. In fact, it seems almost silly to discuss spiritual warfare in relation to Wicca and Satanism, since there are more tempting and equally dangerous temptations.

*We have to expect spiritual warfare.* To expect otherwise ensures spiritual frustration, a consistently fearful believer, and certain spiritual failure. However, expecting warfare doesn't mean looking for wars to fight. It also doesn't mean hiding when we know we're in the midst of a war.

Believers either hide by running from the attack (by avoidance or giving in), or they hide through prayer, asking for prayer while often not really dealing with the actual attack. The other way believers attempt spiritual warfare is to actually go on the attack against what they believe is attacking them. Unfortunately, this is often done by hitting first. Believers often make up untruths about Wiccans and Satanists. They often use forceful evangelistic techniques, doing more to turn off the opposing adherent. This method of spiritual warfare has created hatred for Christians. As if our message wasn't controversial enough to people who haven't heard the gospel, Wiccans and Satanists often can't stand us because we've attacked them.

I suggest that spiritual warfare is often not what we believe it is. Believers have grown accustomed to thinking that spiritual warfare always involves demons, emotional depression, moral failure, etc. And, in fact, I believe that these are actual forms of spiritual warfare. We know that Satan desires to see us wounded and depressed and even beaten (see 1 Peter 5:8, and Revelation 2:10, for example). And we know that Satan will use anything, including demons, to accomplish this (see 1 Timothy 4:1–2 and Matthew 8 as examples of demonic attack). However, these are not always the norm. Spiritual attack is more often subtle, and passes under the radar of the most devout adherent.

Our mindset about spiritual warfare must change. We have to be aware of the subtly of Satan, and refocus our attention on the ordinary, daily influence of spiritual forces, beliefs, ideas, and practices that we are confronted with daily. The most effective lie Satan has perpetuated among believers today is to teach that spiritual warfare is in the huge tragedies. In fact, the most effective war Satan wages against believers is in the subtle influence we often don't notice. Paul closes the first part of his famous passage on spiritual warfare with the word, "Stand." This word is an infinitive word. It implies an ongoing stand. The message from Paul's mind, rippling through history to believers today is to continue to stand in all circumstances and situations. Be constantly aware of the subtle influences, so that our walk does not waiver.

## THE CALL TO ALL PEOPLE

John, stuck on the island of Patmos at an old age, must have heard about the fear in the early church. Persecution and challenges from other religions had tested these believers Jesus gave his beloved disciple a vision and understanding of what the future held. John wrote this revelation to encourage believers. You probably know well the words, pictures and metaphors in the Revelation of John. The end, however, paints John's understanding of the end times and the results of the end times on the lives of all people. At the end of his revelation, John writes:

> Behold, I am coming soon! My reward is with me, and I will give to everyone according to what he has done. I am the Alpha and the Omega, the First and the Last the Beginning and the End. . . . The spirit and the bride say, "Come!" And let him who hears say, "Come!" Whoever is thirsty, let him come; and whoever wishes, let him take the free gift of the water of life. (Revelation 22:12–13, 17)

Throughout this book, we've seen that spiritually thirsty people will do whatever they can to quench their thirst. Because they don't want to submit to God's laws, they will create beliefs and understandings of the world that seem rational and reasonable. We should not be surprised. When you remove God from the framework of his creation, humans begin grasping at straws, trying to make sense of life.

John's words are a call throughout time to all of humanity. Ultimately, this answers the passion of Wicca and Satanism. These two religions have demonstrated their thirstiness and their desire to drink from the mirage they've created. Left alone, Wiccans and Satanists are completely and utterly lost. Their disgust for the laws of God, and their unwillingness to acknowledge the Creator leads them toward a dismal eternity.

The attitude of the Christian has to be the attitude expressed by Jesus at the end of his Word, "Whoever is thirsty, drink!" Jesus' words aren't qualified with "Drink, unless you're a Wiccan," or, "Don't go near the cup if you're a Satanist." This free gift is for all, no matter what they've done. No matter what idols they've touched. No matter what spells they've cast. No matter what rituals they've performed.

Christians must live with this attitude. We can't shun the person who believes differently. Even though Wicca and Satanism are beliefs that seem abhorrent, our perspective must be redemptive. We must be the hands and feet of Christ, constantly reaching toward people of all beliefs with the truth that Jesus is available to all people of all faiths in all walks of life. Jesus is for the thirsty, and we are the ones who offer him as the Water of Life.[1]

# BATTLE

## *For Further Study*

*J*ared was wrapping up his story when there was a knock at the door. Everyone jumped.

Mitch walked over to the door and asked, "Who is it?"

"It's me, Mitch. Shelby. Can I come in?"

Mitch opened the door and looked around. "Sure. Come on in."

"My mom told me what was going on. I'm so sorry you're leaving. I wish you'd change your mind. Is Mary here?"

Mitch stepped aside and pointed her to the living room.

When she entered the room, she looked around and saw that everyone was there. This was going to be too easy. Then she noticed Mary. "What happened to you? What's going on here?" Shelby's eyes darted from face to face.

They quickly filled Shelby in on the latest developments. Mitch concluded by saying, "It looks like I was the target of a spiritual battle, and Satan won. I guess I was too weak," he said feeling defeated. "But Shelby, you and the guys are in danger, too. We're leaving town, so we should be safe. But you need to go straight to your dad and tell him everything you guys know. He'll be able to keep you safe."

"I wouldn't be too sure about that," Shelby responded. "I was over at Steph's house before I came here. We were supposed to go to the movies together. Steph told me that they were in the middle of a family crisis, so she wouldn't be able to go. But before she closed the door, her mom walked by, talking on the phone. She mentioned something about Jared and a room, then I heard the name, McCorkles, and Potts and 7:00, then the door closed. I didn't think much about it at the time. Now that I've heard the whole story, I think we are all still in danger. My dad won't do anything based on hearsay. Unless they've physically harmed one of us, there's nothing he can do."

"Shelby's right," Mitch said. "I think I'd better go to Potts tonight and check it out. I need to be able to give Collins some hard evidence, before he can act. I'll take my video camera with me."

"We're going with you," Paul volunteered.

"No, it's too dangerous," Mitch cautioned.

"Hey, we're just as involved as you are. We're going," Paul argued.

Mitch looked around the room. Shelby, Jared, and Mary were nodding. "Mary, I can't control what the others do, but you aren't going. You've already been through enough," Mitch said.

"Dad, I have to do this. I refuse to be scared."

"Okay, but you stay beside me the whole time," Mitch conceded.

Mitch looked at Sandy. "Why don't you pack a few suitcases so we can leave tomorrow? I'll hire a moving company in the morning."

Mitch stood to get a few things together. "I want everyone back here at 5:00. Wear dark clothes."

⁂

UP IN HER room, Mary tried to bolster her confidence. Reading her Bible didn't suppress her fear. Pulling out her diary, she wrote:

Dear Diary, or, To Whom It May Concern,
    I'm scared. I'm writing this in case my dad is wrong, and I don't make it out of Clarke City alive.

Looking back, we were so stupid to get involved in all this. I guess we were involved long before we realized it, but still, I think we may have made things worse.

Right now, all I want to do is find a bed in a place where no one knows me, pull the covers up around my head and hide forever. Even after what we've seen, my dad says that we have to fight this. I guess he's right. If this can happen in Clarke City, it can happen anywhere . . ."

Mary wrote every detail about the Denver Street house. Every encounter she'd had with Steph. All the fear, depression, and loneliness she'd been living with. All the ways she and her family and friends had been affected.

An hour and several pages later, Mary read back what she'd been through. What was God teaching her through all of this? Why would He let her experience all of this?

To console herself and try to give the whole experience some kind of meaning, Mary tried to soldier out a conclusion.

"So tonight, it will all be over. We'll either be driving out of Clarke City forever, or we'll all be dead. Protect me tonight, Jesus. Hold me close. Let me feel your arms around me. Protect Paul, Jared, and Dad too. Let us see you conquer Satan tonight.

"I love you, Mom. Thanks for teaching me about God and for listening. You've been the best mom ever."

Mary closed her diary and placed it in the center of her desk. If she didn't live through this, her mom would certainly find it.

THE WOODS AROUND the clearing were cloaked in evil. A heaviness hung in the air, making it difficult to breathe. The group arrived at 5:30 to get set up. Finding a good hiding spot in some thick brush, they knelt to pray. Mitch led them in a prayer of protection, pleading the blood of Christ on each of them.

As soon as darkness fell around Potts, lights began to appear on the horizon. Mitch pushed record on his camera.

"What's the deal with the torches," Jared whispered.

"Dunno," Paul answered. "But you can bet they aren't trying to hide this time."

"What do you mean?" Mitch looked concerned. "Isn't this what happened the last time you were here?"

"No, last time, they brought candles," Paul said.

"Yeah, and there was a feeling of celebration about it. This time . . . I don't know . . . it feels different some how. Almost like . . ." Mary's voice trailed off as the circle was being cast.

A woman entered the circle leading a hooded person by a rope around the neck.

"Can you tell who that is?" Mitch said."

"It wasn't like this the last time. They didn't do this," was all Mary could say. Her heart was racing.

The coven encircled the woman and the hooded person. Standing in the center, the woman began the ceremony.

"Many years ago, when we came to this city there was no opposition. We could practice in peace. But the enemy has grown. They have grown in power. They have grown in wisdom. They have learned too much."

"In this ceremony we present this symbolic sacrifice. She stands in the place of the enemy. Brothers and sisters, thank this one taken from another body for being the substitution. Thank her for being willing to be the connection between us and the enemy."

The chorus of voices raised in proclamation. "Thank you, willing sacrifice." Their voices droned, almost mechanical.

The leader knelt in the center of the group at the feet of the hooded sacrifice. She continued.

"Great Spirit, we beseech thee. Come and fill our circle. We join power tonight with another path for our own common good. Make our power . . ." The woman stopped and stood. She searched the faces of the coven, looking for someone. "There are spirits here." Her voice was biting, her gaze piercing. "There is one like us but on a different path. With her are other spirits. Angry spirits."

Glancing at Shelby, Mitch noticed her necklace. It was a small wooden pentagram. As he studied Shelby's necklace, he noticed her face. Something was different. She was not the girl he came to know a year ago when she began coming to RealWalk. She looked older, wiser. The innocence was gone from her eyes.

Without saying anything, Shelby stood. The woman leading the mock sacrifice called out. "Daughter Shelby," smiling proudly. "I feel your energy."

"Brothers and sisters, one week ago, we welcomed Sister Shelby into our coven. Those of you who were there remember the beautiful ceremony and her amazing spirit."

The group nodded and looked at Shelby.

"She has chosen a parallel path—one like ours, but different. And yet, her spirit is devoted to our craft. We welcome her as a sister tonight, for she has helped reveal the enemy to us."

"Yes, sister. I've done what was asked of me. See?" Shelby pointed to the group around her, looking for praise and affirmation. The group was barely visible to the coven, but they could be seen. Mitch, Mary, Jared, and Paul looked up at Shelby. They couldn't believe what she was doing. This was a nightmare. How could they not know that Shelby had joined a coven?

Rick came to the center of the group and joined his wife who had been leading the ceremony. "Dear friends," he began. "If it takes a lifetime we will raise up a generation of children from this city who walk the ancient path. The opposing force hiding in the woods seeks to prevent us from accomplishing our task. They are the reason we're here tonight."

Suddenly, the appearance of a dark spirit hovered above each member of the coven. It was an indefinite shape of black mist. The more Rick spoke, the more pronounced the shapes above each witch became. A breeze filled the clearing as the misty spirits gently floated higher, then lower. They were riding the breeze just above their human hosts. They hissed and moaned with envy and excitement.

Rick continued the ceremony, taking a large silver dagger and holding it above his head. "Kneel," Rick commanded. The subject knelt. Rick walked behind the person, grabbed her head, and pulled it back, exposing the throat. With each movement, the spirit hovered above Rick and grew larger, fiercer. The wind moved its smoky form.

"We join together tonight many paths with one purpose. Help us, we pray. Help us conquer the opposing spirits," Rick said. He shouted so the coven could hear him above the wind; so the trees could hear him; so the spirits could hear; so the enemy hiding in the woods could hear him.

Rick lowered the dagger to the throat of the victim. He placed the flat side of the blade against her throat.

"Powers of the South, Power of Fire, fill us. Powers of the West, Power of Water, give us strength . . ."

He slowly drew the dagger across the throat of the victim.

The spirit grew larger. It hissed and began to move. In, then out. Slowly. Like an old man taking long, deep breaths.

Rick held the dagger above the head of the kneeling victim. "Rid us of the enemy! Rid us of the enemy!" Rick said over and over, his voice increasing in volume with each statement.

The spirit grew, hissing and moaning. It shoved at the other spirits, constantly moving. It filled the area above the coven, forming a black covering over each witch and each of the obviously lesser spirits. The spirits cowered, but never moved from their human hosts.

Rick pretended to thrust the dagger repeatedly into the stomach of the kneeling victim. With each stab, Rick yelled, "Rid us!" The coven repeated his yell.

Mitch and the kids still hugged the ground, unable to move. A heaviness fell over them. With each cycle, the spirit grew even larger, covering everything in the area until the rocks, trees, grass, and even the air slowly became part of the spirit, completely taken in by it.

"Do you feel that?" Jared asked. "I feel like there are a billion hands pushing at me all at once."

"Yeah, like you're being pushed into a little ball," Paul added, "and someone is going to keep pushing you until . . ."

"Until you don't exist anymore?" Mitch finished.

"Exactly."

The thickness of the spirit was so great that the group stood to look around, no longer afraid that the coven would see them. This spirit was far more dangerous than the coven. The area around them was as thick as a dense, black fog that was somehow alive. Whispering in their ears, the group heard the fog hissing, moaning.

Suddenly, there was a flash. What was once a single spirit empowered to fulfill one purpose had become thirty spirits, all with one common goal. They hovered over Mitch and the group.

In the center of the coven, Rick spoke. "We release you to your work. With reverence and awe, we wait."

Most of the coven ran into the woods. Rick and several others of the devoted members stood watching the Christians. "See, I told you," he said in a raspy whisper. "We have them! Patience. All we need is a little patience. This will all be over soon."

The chaos continued. In the midst of the confusion, Mary found herself standing face to face with the hooded person who was unable to move because of the ropes. Mary looked at the person, and reaching for the hood, pulled it off.

Mary stared Steph in the face. Above Steph, a spirit hovered. Black. Angry. Demanding. Mary stared at it, and its angry mocking face stared down at her. Mary could feel its thoughts.

"I told you, Mary. We'll win this. I told you that you had no idea what you were dealing with," Steph taunted. "We have joined," she continued, "the old path with the new. This is new for all of us. We're learning to accept our differences. You will too. You have no choice."

Mary caught a glimpse of her dad wrestling with something on the ground. She couldn't tell if Mitch had control of it, or if it had control of Mitch. They were wrestling so fiercely that the two looked like they were becoming the same person. The more they wrestled, the more substance the demon had.

"Dad!" Mary yelled over to her father. "Remember the prayer! Pray the rescue prayer!"

As soon as the words left her lips, Mitch began praying, each word rushing urgently out of his mouth.

"Jesus! Protect me! Give me your strength." Suddenly there was a definite separation of Mitch and the demon. Mitch was able to shove it off him. The two continued to struggle. The demon kept slashing at Mitch's mouth trying to prevent him from praying. He pushed his hand into Mitch's mouth.

"Jesus! Surround me with angels!" Mitch croaked out, barely able to speak through the demon's hand.

Suddenly, there was a pop. A black dust filled the air.

Silence.

The coven had run off. Mitch sat up, touching the back of his hand to his mouth. It was bleeding. The demon that was on top of him had disappeared. The hissing and moaning of the black smoky spirits was gone. Alone in the clearing, Mitch, Mary, Jared, and Paul heard sirens in the distance.

"Did we win, dad?"

"I wouldn't say win, Mary, but we're safe for now."

"What happened?" Jared asked, his mind beginning to clear.

"I think we finally saw what we're up against," Mitch said, his voice ringing with a cautious confidence.

Shaken from the battle, the small group stood and brushed themselves off.

"Hold it right there. Don't move!" a voice commanded. Several spotlights were aimed at their faces. It was Chief Collins.

Sirens and lights filled the clearing. Sandy pushed past the officers and ran to her family. Wrapping her arms around Mary, she looked up at Mitch. "I'm sorry, but I couldn't just stay at home hoping for you to arrive. It took a lot of fast talking, but I finally convinced Chief Collins to come out here."

Mitch embraced Sandy. "I've got the whole thing caught on video," Mitch said, pointing to a video camera on a tripod, standing in the woods, across the clearing. "I hope it'll help you in your investigation."

"I'll check it out later. Paul, Jared, let me take you home. I need to talk to your parents."

Mitch, Mary, and Sandy drove back to their house. "What now?" Sandy asked, looking at Mitch and Mary.

"Collins has the tape. I say we wait until we hear from him. Let's get home. I still need to call that moving company."

"I thought you were dead back there, Dad."

"Me too. We couldn't see his angels, but we certainly felt them, huh?"

"I never thought I'd see you again," Sandy said, wiping her eyes.

"God is good," Mitch said confidently. "God is so good."

# EPILOGUE

*W*e've been on quite a journey, haven't we? Looking back over this book, I am reminded of the lengths people will take to avoid accepting God's love and submitting to his guidance. Why is it that we humans refuse the hand of the Loving Creator in our lives? What makes us flee from God, when he is our only hope? Why do we think that we can create our own religious system and belief?

My hope is that through this book you've seen the differences between Wicca and Satanism, and how much they differ from Christianity. I hope you've seen that Wicca and Satanism look a lot alike because they really are a lot alike. I've tried to do this honestly, without putting down Wiccans or Satanists, and without just saying "because the Bible says so." Most of all, I've tried to show this through reporting to you from their sources, hoping that you'll see the differences between these beliefs and Christianity.

Witchcraft and Satanism are huge subjects. There isn't any way one book can adequately cover every detail about these beliefs. So for your further study (and possibly for your edification) the following are points that lead to a broader study of Wiccan and Satanism. We didn't deal with them in this book, but should you want a further understanding of witchcraft and Satanism, I recommend the following subjects, beliefs, and ideas to you. A discussion on these is easily found either in a bookstore, or by using an Internet search engine.

One word of caution: Be careful. Should you choose to search further in these topics you'll encounter some pretty weird things. The deeper you get, the more dangerous material you'll encounter.

I hope this book has been a help to you. God bless you as you further discover the mysteries of these religions. It's my prayer that through further knowledge of these subjects that you'll be more grounded in Christ Jesus, and will be able to further glorify him in your life.

## Wicca

- The religions of Ancient Mesopotamia are more varied than I have described them here. They're interesting to study to get a broader grasp of how the ancient mind understood the world.

- Some Wiccan scholars trace the beginning of society (and religious belief) to India, and work their way forward to establish that religion has always included a mother/father godhead. This study has some interesting archaeological support.

- A close relative of Wicca is voodoo. Studying this religion and practice will help give a broader perspective of how Wicca is understood in the world today.

- The idea of Pagan religions is broader than I have painted it in this book. There have been many competing religions over the years that could be classified as "Pagan." Knowing more about these religions would offer a broader understanding of Wicca.

- Many scholars believe that the biblical understanding of heaven and hell came from ancient Greece. Knowing the ancient understanding of the afterlife might give further detail to what heaven is really like.

• Wiccans describe the Salem witch trials in both England and the United States as a time of great religious persecution. Many people were killed for allegedly practicing witchcraft. Entire volumes of books have been written on these subjects. Many scholars disagree about what happened at the trials and how many people were actually killed. This is an interesting segment of history in the development of witchcraft. It would be worth your time to know more about it.

• Divination practices like tarot, automatic writing, and others are rooted deep in Wicca, and are present in other religions as well. These might be interesting studies.

## SATANISM

• The occult was largely developed within ancient Egyptian religions which continues to influence Satanism. A deeper study will help in better understanding Satanism today.

• Scholars believe that the biblical idea of Satan is derived from ancient cultures. Knowing what they thought of the "darker side of humanity" will help in grasping this.

• An emerging religious spin-off from Satanism is modern-day vampires. Studing this slant on Satanic thought might offer a broader understanding of Satanism.

• There are many symbols (including the Star of David) used by Satanists in ritual and worship. Knowing these will help in noticing Satanic influences in our society.

• Satanic ritual has been used to explain the discovery of butchered animals used in what appears to be occult worship. This area of study would be easy to research.

• The works of H.P. Lovecraft and others are influenced by satanic worship. Much information exists about these writers and how their beliefs influenced their writings.

## GENERAL

• Modern media blends Wicca, Satanism, and other beliefs into a mysterious religion that practices witchcraft, conjures demons, etc. What is being promoted today doesn't adequately fit into either Wicca or Satanism. Further study of modern media and its use of these beliefs might be of use.

• Many of the Wiccan holidays and celebrations are believed to have influenced the early church. In fact, many of our Christian celebrations appear to have been influenced by early Pagan, Celt, and Wiccan holidays. Each Christian holiday has a neat history, and it would be worth it to know more about them.

# Chapter 17

# UNTIL THE END

*C*ollins eased back into his chair, remote in hand, studying Mitch's videotape. He watched it a few times, then forwarded it to the ending several times. The confused look on his face didn't bode well for Mitch and the kids.

"I'm not sure what he's talking about," Collins' secretary said. "I don't see anything except Mitch leading a crazy group of kids around in the woods terrorizing people."

"See what I mean?" a voice chimed in from across the office. Pastor Rick stood holding statements from the Pattersons about how Jared broke into their garage and rummaged through a private room. Another statement came from Stephanie about how Mary made false claims about her promiscuity at school. There were other statements from the elders of C4 about how Mitch became the Pied Piper of the church and led many kids away from God.

"We were meeting in the woods and all of the sudden, they just attacked." Rick's words streamed out easily.

Collins studied the video closer. "Mitch said there were demons or spirits or something. There's nothing like that here. I'm going to need to talk to Mitch."

"You should," Rick responded. "We can't allow Mitch to harm others, no matter what he believes. I'm hoping for your support on this, Collins. Can I count on you to make this right for our church?"

"You bet, Rick. I'm sorry I didn't believe you before. We'll get Mitch back in here for some more questioning. I'm sure he'll confess after we prove to him that he's lying."

"I'm exhausted," Rick said, plopping into the chair next to Collins' secretary. "You and Marcie want to come over for dinner tonight? I can invite the Pattersons too. Maybe we could talk about our strategy for confronting Mitch."

"Sounds great, Rick. I know Shelby will want to come. How about 6:00? I'll have Marcie bring a salad?

"Great! See you then."

※

IN THE BASEMENT of the Denver Street house, Shelby leaned over a notebook. Candles covered the homemade altar set diagonally in the corner of the damp room. Red. Black. Green. The candles provided the only light in the room. The smell of fire mixed with incense. The walls were covered with symbols—pentagrams and copies of ancient writings. This was the house where it all started, but this time, they were in the basement. This was the room Steph's coven had met in for years, their place of freedom.

Shelby wrote in her book of shadows. Her charcoal pencil moved rhythmically across the page. The words were dictated to her by Steph.

"Write this," she said. "Write it exactly like I say . . ."

One sentence at a time, Steph offered the words.

"Commit yourself to him. Say it like this . . ."

"Almighty Master, today I give you my life. I commit to the way of confusion."

Shelby wrote as Steph spoke. The words became her words.

"Tell him what you want. Tell him what you want your life to mean." Steph's directions sounded pastoral. Leading. Encouraging.

"Above all, make me like you. As others have gone before me, make me your leader. Let your power help me lead others into darkness. All hail you, my prince."

Just as it was for Steph and those before her, now it is for Shelby. As one believed, so one passed it down to their disciple. It had always been this way. It would never end.

# NOTES

CHAPTER 1—The Old Religion
1. Margot Adler, *Drawing Down the Moon* (New York: Penguin Books, 1986), 46.
2. James Prichard, *The Ancient Near East* (New Jersey: Princeton University Press, 1973), 31ff.

CHAPTER 2—The Interesting Lie
1. Bart Ehrman, *A Brief Introduction to the New Testament,* page 21.
2. Raymond Buckland, *The Witch Book* (Michigan: Visible Ink, 2002), 81.
3. For some more information on this section, check out the book "The Almanac of the Uncanny" noted on the web at www.celticcallings.com/resources/celtic_traditions/the_druids.htm.

CHAPTER 4—Morality and The Rede
1. http://www.xeper.org/maquino/nm/COS.pdf. 437.
2. http://www.churchofsatan.com/Pages/Eleven.html.

CHAPTER 5—Pentagrams and Baphomets
1. Buckland, *The Witch Book,* 148.
2. Buckland, *The Witch Book,* 297.
3. Buckland, *The Witch Book,* 37.
4. http://www.xeper.org/maquino/nm/COS.pdf. 566.
5. http://www.churchofsatan.com/Pages/BaphometSigil.html.

CHAPTER 6—Magic
1. Buckland, *The Witch Book,* 312-313.
2. Raven Grimassi, *The Spirit of the Witch* (Minnesota: Llewellyn Publications, 2003), 48-49.

3. http://www.xeper.org/maquino/nm/COS.pdf. 438.
4. Tim Baker, *Why So Many Gods?*, 156-160.

CHAPTER 7—The Evolution of Humanity
1. http://www.xeper.org/maquino/nm/COS.pdf. 542.

CHAPTER 8—Worlds and Planes
1. These seven planes of existence are gleaned from Raven Grimassi, *The Spirit of the Witch*, 150-152.

CHAPTER 11—Covens
1. Buckland, *The Witch Book*, 99.
2. Raymond Buckland, *The Complete Book of Witchcraft* (Minnesota: Llewellyn Publications, 2003), 80.
3. http://www.xeper.org/maquino/nm/COS.pdf. 584-585 and 821-822.

CHAPTER 13—The Bible and Witchcraft
1. Donald Redford, *The Ancient Gods Speak* (New York: Oxford University Press, 2002), 30-32 and 80-82.
2. Bruce Metzger, *Oxford Companion to the Bible* (New York: Oxford University Press, 1993), 368.

CHAPTER 15—Tying Up Loose Ends
1. There are many books that specifically direct believers in the specifics of how to craft their testimony and message to unbelievers. As a primer on the basics of witnessing, try my book *Witnessing 101* (Transit Books). This resource offers valuable information on basic Christian beliefs, shaping a testimony, and how to approach unbelievers (including Wiccans and Satanists) with the Gospel.

# BIBLIOGRAPHY

$A$s with any study of witchcraft and the occult, great care must be taken when reading and researching. Some resources and internet sites contain objectionable images and material.

BOOKS

Adler, Margot, *Drawing Down the Moon*. New York: Penguin Books. 1986.

Buckland, Raymond, *The Witch Book*. Michigan: Visible Ink. 2002.

Buckland, Raymond, *Buckland's Complete Book of Witchcraft*. Minnesota: Llewellyn Publications. 2003.

Drew, A.J., *A Wiccan Bible*. New Jersey: New Page Books. 2003.

Grimassi, Raven, *Spirit of the Witch*. Minnesota: Llewellyn Publications. 2003.

McDowell, Josh, *Handbook of Today's Religions*. California: Here's Life Publishers. 1983.

Metzger, Bruce, *The Oxford Companion to the Bible*. New York: Oxford University Press. 1993.

Moura, Ann, *Origins of Modern Witchcraft*. Minnesota: Llewellyn Publications. 2002.

Prichard, James, *The Ancient Near East* New Jersey: Princeton University Press. 1973.

Redford, Donald, *The Ancient Gods Speak: A guide to Egyptian religion*. New York: Oxford University Press. 2002.

Simkins, Ronald, *Creator and Creation: Nature in the Worldview of Ancient Israel*. Massachusetts: Hendrickson Publishers. 1994.

Smart, Ninian, *The Religious Experience of Mankind.* New York: Scribner and Sons Publishing. 1984.

Smith, Mark, *The Early History of God.* Michigan: Eerdmans Publishing. 2002.

Thomas, D. Winton, *Documents from Old Testament Times.* New York: Harper Torchbook. 1961.

## INTERNET RESOURCES

Many of these internet sites offer a wealth of information on Wicca and Satanism, their influences, and how they've influenced others. In many cases I've listed the general site as a source.

### WICCA

www.wicca.org

www.wicca.com

www.wicca.net

www.branwenscauldron.com/witch_wicca.html

www.cog.org

www.newadvent.org/cathen/15674a.htm

www.pantheon.org/areas/featured/witchcraft

www.witchvox.com/basics

www.witchway.net/wicca/what4.html

http://home.ptd.net/~wolfen/compare/compare.htm

### CELTS AND PAGANS

www.sacred-texts.com/neu/celt/rac

www.celticcallings.com/resources/celtic_traditions/celtic_relgion.htm

www.celticcallings.com/resources/celtic_traditions/a_brief_history.htm

www.celticcallings.com/resources/celtic_traditions/the_druids.htm

www.newadvent.org/cathen/11388a.htm

www.bloomington.in.us/~pen/mwcraft.html

http://home.ptd.net/~wolfen/compare/d&w.html

### SATANISM

www.xper.org

www.churchofsatan.com

www.exposingsatanism.org

www.spiritwatch.org/sattruth.htm

www.vampiretemple.com

www.luckymojo.com/faqs/faq.astnngp.9907

www.answers.org/Satan/Sra.html

www.dpjs.co.uk/serpent.html
www.rotten.com/library/bio/religion/aleister-crowley

NECRONOMICON
www.geocities.com/SoHo/9879/necgloss.htm
www.ping.de/sites/systemcoder/necro/info/text1.htm
www.necfiles.org/voynich.htm
http://users.resentment.org/devilmiyu/tome.html

RITUALS
www.satanicrituals.com

DIVINATION
www.salemtarot.com/tarothistory.html
www.sacred-texts.com/tarot

For study guides, or more information on
Wicca, Witchcraft, and Satanism go to
*www.dewitched.com*

To contact Tim Baker for speaking,
email him at tim@dewitched.com
or visit *www.timbaker.cc*